PUZZLE OF PONIES

MARY GERVAISE

Armada

First published in the U.K. in 1964 by
Lutterworth Press, London. This edition was first
published in 1974 by Armada Books
14 St. James's Place, London S.W.1.

Printed in Great Britain by
Love & Malcomson Ltd.,
Brighton Road, Redhill, Surrey.

*Facilities for the cover photograph kindly provided by
The Moat House, Benenden, Kent.*

CONTENTS

1.	Tuning Up	7
2.	Burnt Bacon	17
3.	Over the Bridge	27
4.	The Gate-Crashers	39
5.	Police!	49
6.	On the Way!	60
7.	The Fun of the Fair	67
8.	Surprise Item	79
9.	To Make Amends	89
10.	The Secret	97
11.	Daylight	107
12.	The End Of It All	118

CHAPTER ONE

TUNING UP

"Now this is what I call snug," Georgie said with a contented sigh, as she lay back in her father's big chair and gazed at the crackling log fire. King Toby, her beautiful orange cat, who was curled up on top of her, gave an extra loud purr to show that he agreed.

Rough and Tough, Georgie's twin brothers, and Velvet and Plush, their twin spaniels, were reclining in a heap on the hearth rug, while Susan Walker, her best friend, was balancing on the arm of the settee, extracting terrible sounds from a recorder. Seventeen-year-old Peter was the eldest of the Kane family, being two years older than the twins, and three years older than Georgie. He was endeavouring to read a historical magazine through the general hubbub. Peter was a little hampered by the fact that his mother, who was knitting him a pullover, kept on wanting to measure various parts of him. The most elegant and composed person in the room was neat, fair-haired Geraldine Holden, the Kanes' cousin, who was the same age as Georgie. She was sitting in a straight-backed chair, embroidering her monogram on a new handkerchief.

"Snug's the word," said Susan, nodding her bright red head. "Pheep, pheep, pheee! Er—would you recognize that as *Strawberry Fair*, Mrs. Kane? Oh, well, I only got the recorder yesterday—I mean, even great musicians have to practise . . . Listen to the wind! Isn't it lovely to be indoors on a night like this, with a fire and everything? Pheep!"

"The first fire of autumn. It's almost as exciting as the first tea in the garden, in spring," Georgie said dreamily. Her big hazel eyes were shining with happiness as she reflected that there was still a week left of the summer holidays.

It had been a busy summer. Georgie, Susan, and Gerry had been staying with friends at Whitelea, where in an amateur gymkhana Georgie's pony Spot had won his first rosette. Mr. and Mrs. Kane had been to Paris, and the boys had stayed with their own friends. Now they were all home again, and ready to make the most of these last few days.

"A whole week of peace!" said Susan. "And we've jolly well earned it, too. Pheep, pheep——"

"Sue dear, do forget about music for a moment," said Mrs. Kane, giving Peter an absent-minded prod with a knitting needle. "I agree with Georgie—it *is* snug to be here by our own fireside while the wind howls round the house. But when you say snug's the word—make sure it isn't *smug*, instead. Nobody earns a week of peace merely by having a jolly good time!"

"And Spot's rosette was only for being the Best-tempered Pony," Gerry remarked rather sourly. "He didn't *do* anything . . ."

Georgie flushed, for she knew that Spot, her beautiful chestnut pony who hadn't a spot on him anywhere, had done a great deal that summer. Once she would have flared up at Gerry's unkind statement, but she had learnt a great deal of self-control lately.

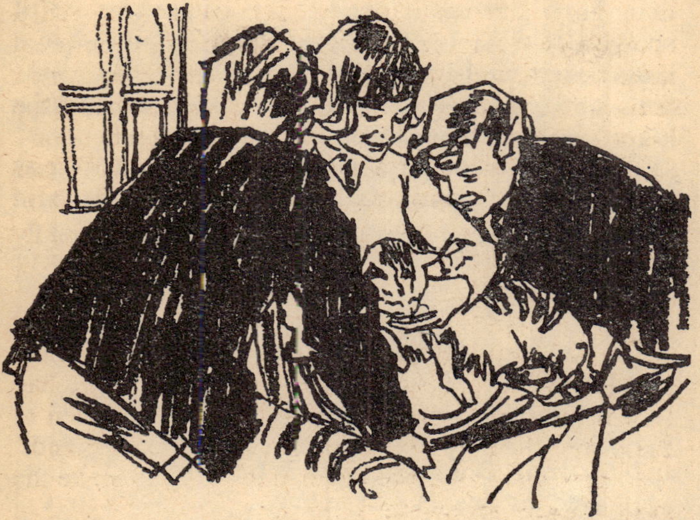

"How can I get out of his chair without disturbing this mountain of fur?"

"Smug's a horrible word," she said emphatically, "and a horrible thing to be. I didn't mean that, at least I hope I didn't. I was just purring really, like King Toby. Oh, I can hear Daddy coming back. What a long time he's been on the 'phone! How can I get out of his chair without disturbing this mountain of fur?"

"Keep still, then," said Tough.

"And stop breathing," said Rough, and together the twins rose and lifted their sister out of the chair and on to the rug, without putting Toby to the slightest inconvenience. In fact, he didn't bother to open his eyes.

Georgie, laughing with the rest, looked up from her lowly position and saw her father come into the room. His face was so grave that she knew at once that something important had happened. She realized before he spoke that what he was going to say would have a lasting effect on them all.

Georgie's mother knew it too. "What is it?" she asked quickly. "Is anyone ill?"

"No one belonging to us," Mr. Kane answered at once, "but I'm afraid the Duponts are having a bad time. They want us to help them, my dear, and I really think we must."

"What's happened—an accident?" asked Rough.

"Can't be," Tough said at once. "There hasn't been time."

Mr. and Mrs. Kane's Paris holiday had ended, as all the family knew, in their going to stay with Monsieur and Madame Dupont and their three small children, who lived in one of the suburbs. Mr. Kane was a hydraulic engineer, and Monsieur Dupont, though much younger, belonged to the same firm. He was in England now on business, and had in fact flown over with Mr. and Mrs. Kane.

"Accidents don't take so very long to happen," Mr. Kane said now, smiling wryly at the twins, "and I'm afraid they've had a bad one. Jacques came over with us, as you may remember, and Mélanie came by boat the day after, bringing the children and the car. She joined Jacques in London and they all drove up to Shadow Water, in the Lake District, because he wanted to show her that dam we built two years ago. And they had a collision with a lorry. It was Jacques's own fault, I'm afraid. He forgot about driving on the left. And now he's in hospital with a fractured leg, and Mélanie's with the children at the cottage where several of us stayed when we were working there; but she has a sprained ankle and a wrist in plaster, and the eldest child is three!"

"Oh, *dear*!" said Mrs. Kane, aghast, "and the cottage is right on the banks of the lake; the children will be tumbling in. The elderly couple who own it couldn't possibly cope with them. Poor Mélanie!" She went across to her husband. "Was it she who rang up?" she asked. "Does she want us to find a hotel?"

"No, it was the doctor from the hospital," he answered. "Jacques asked him to ring me. After all, we're their only friends in England. He's desperately worried about it all. The doctor said Mélanie ought to be in hospital herself, but she wouldn't—couldn't—leave the kids. He asked if we'd go up there . . ."

"I knew it!" said Gerry. "I think it's awful! Whenever things go wrong, people make use of you, Aunt Marcia and Uncle John—and it's so unfair. Why did Madame Dupont have to come over at all, with those children? Now you'll go, I suppose, and the last week of the hols will be all upset. *I* know!"

"Oh, Gerry," said Mrs. Kane, "when things like this happen one doesn't bother to work out whose fault it is. Still, we don't want to be away for the last week. John!" she exclaimed, "suppose we go up to Shadow Water tomorrow, and bring Mélanie and the children back with us?"

There was a moment of stunned silence, and then Mr. Kane said something about elastic walls. Wychwood was not a small house, but every available bed was in use at present

"The vicar would lend us extra beds," Mrs. Kane declared. "There are at least four spare bedrooms at the vicarage which are never used."

"Couldn't Mrs. Dupont and the kids sleep there,

then?" Susan and Gerry cried at the same instant, a suggestion which Mr. Kane had to turn down.

"They're our responsibility," he said. "I'll ring the vicarage now. And if it's all right, as it's sure to be, we'll go up to Cumberland tomorrow, my dear. That will be Friday. I suggest that we spend Saturday and Sunday at Shadow Water, as I'd like to see Jacques, of course, and do some business as well with the local engineering firm which gave us so much help with the dam. Then we could come home peacefully on Monday with our cargo."

"That means leaving the children for a whole week-end," said Mrs. Kane, with sudden misgivings, but of course she was howled down.

"Children!" Georgie exploded. "Mother, you'd be surprised if you knew what our united ages amounted to."

"Do *you* know?" Gerry asked pointedly, as mathematics were not Georgie's strongest subject. "All the same, Aunt Marcia," she went on calmly, "there's absolutely no need for you to worry about us. If six responsible human beings can't manage to look after themselves——"

"And a cat, a pony, and two dogs," Susan murmured.

"For seventy-two hours," Gerry continued imperturbably, "they deserve to be marooned on a desert island, that's all I can say!"

"Let's hope it is," Susan muttered, but Mrs. Kane, overhearing, shook her head slightly, and Susan subsided.

"You certainly make it sound very simple, Gerry," Mr. Kane said, laughing, "and I really don't see that much *could* happen in such a short time. By the way, there's an agricultural show over at Stonebridge, if you can get yourselves there. I was going to drive you over on Saturday, but now you'll have to go by bus."

"Stonebridge?" said the twins in unison. "Where's that?"

"It's a place I've never been through," their father answered. "I've just missed it, somehow. It's the other side of Driscoe, going away from the moors. There's rather a famous bridge there, over the river Cara, which is a tributary of the Tamar. I think there's a castle as well. Still, the show may not appeal to you. It's not as if it were near enough for Georgie and Sue to ride over, and *compete*."

"Oh, Daddy!" Georgie looked scandalized. "I couldn't ride in a real show, and Sue couldn't on Timbo. She might if she had Aggie."

Susan sighed. Aggie was Black Agnes, her beloved pony, now spending the summer holidays at the Grange School in High Lennet, in Dorset. The Kanes had hired a neighbouring pony for her, and he was a great success; but of course it wasn't the same.

"In any case," she said, "you have to send your entry in beforehand, and all that. But it would be nice to go to it."

"I believe there's a good play on at the Driscoe Rep," Gerry said pensively. Rough and Tough who were often dubbed The Lads, said something about a Rare Bird Exhibition in Periton.

"It seems as if you and Mother ought to go away for a month, not a mere week-end," Peter said to his father as he looked up from his magazine. "I'll be madly busy all Saturday, writing that treatise on Folk Music which has to be handed in as soon as I get back to school. I'll be on the spot, in case you want to ring up from Shadow Water."

"Oh, good, you'll be able to give King Toby his lunch, then," Georgie said with satisfaction, "and turn the gas on, if we leave a casserole in the oven. I was wondering how we could all go off, now Mrs. Duncan's away."

"Poor careworn housewife!" laughed Mrs. Kane. "I'll ask someone from the village to come in and get the meal." But six indignant voices rose in protest.

"They'll be all right, Marcia. They can forage for themselves for once," said Mr. Kane, "and the casserole idea seems good. After all, it's only for one short weekend!"

Then he went to telephone the elderly vicar about beds, and Mrs. Kane hurried off to make a good stock of cake and sausage rolls and pies, to leave behind for her family.

"It's going to be fabulous!" said Susan. "*Pheep*! Peter, *Strawberry Fair* counts as Folk Music, doesn't it? I'll play it all through, very slowly, to give you atmosphere . . . Phip, phip, phip, PHEEP!"

"Thanks very much, Sue," Peter broke in gently, though with some haste, "but I've roughed out the treatise, you see, so I don't need any atmosphere just now."

"Is that the only tune you know?" asked Gerry. "Or is it simply that you've got it on the brain?" And she was quite obviously about to add that perhaps that was impossible, when Georgie trod meaningly on her toe. She was always having to keep the peace between these two. Sue could be utterly maddening, of course, but she was a far nicer person than Gerry. And yet Georgie, who had always rather disliked her priggish, efficient cousin until a short while ago, could not side with a stranger against her own flesh and blood. There were times when she wished to smack them both.

"I know plenty of tunes, thank you, Gerry," Susan said sweetly, "but *Strawberry Fair* came into my head this afternoon when we were in Driscoe. It was when you were in Cox's buying your saddle soap, Georgie. There were some saddles hanging up outside, and one was a great big hunting saddle, and three men came along and looked at it. And one of them laughed and dug the others in the ribs. 'Reckon I'll be wanting that in a month or two, for my strawberry roan!' he said, and they all guffawed. Horrid, rude creatures!" she ended unexpectedly.

"Why, Sue?" asked Tough lazily. "The best people are allowed to guffaw nowadays!"

"Oh, it wasn't *that*," Susan replied, colouring. "But one of them dropped a bit of paper as they moved on. He didn't notice, so I picked it up for him, and he snatched it from me, and said—I *think* he said—'Nah then, Nosey!' "

"I wish I'd been there," said Peter, rather fiercely.

"Oh, it didn't matter really," grinned Susan, who was always quick to regain her poise, "and I daresay I oughtn't to have read what was written on it."

"Sue!" cried everyone, in righteous wrath, and she shrugged her square shoulders.

"I give up!" she said dramatically. "It's like asking the difference between a secret agent and a spy. There was a word on that piece of paper, and I've memorized it. It may be the password to some hidden treasure."

"Spies and treasure! Really, Susan, how corny can you get?" sniffed Gerry. "And it *was* nosey to read it."

"Huh! If it did happen to be a password, as I was

saying when I was interrupted, Susan paused to glare at Gerry, "I'd have my picture in the papers, and everyone would be thrilled. I might even get a reward, or a medal. But if it's just an ordinary private note, then I'm nosey. How does one *know*?"

"Supper in ten minutes," said Mrs. Kane, from the doorway. "Who'll come and make toast?"

"Me!" cried Susan, forgetting her question, and soon, in the cheerful uproar of the last meal they would have together, the subject of the discussion was forgotten.

CHAPTER TWO

BURNT BACON

GEORGIE was up very early next morning, when heavy dew glittered like jewels on the lawn. She knew her father and mother wanted to start their journey before eight, so she took their breakfast upstairs to them on a tray. They were delighted.

"One good turn deserves another," smiled her father, opening his wallet. "Here's a five pound note. Put it somewhere safe and say nothing about it. Wait till a suitable moment, which is sure to come, and then spend it on something you'll all enjoy."

"Daddy!" She hugged him impulsively. "What a lovely idea. Can it be anything? I mean, if we go to the Stonebridge Show, and there's a fair on, you won't think we've wasted it if we spend some of it on swings?"

"In this case, no," he said decidedly. "It's been given you to enjoy, and as long as it brings real pleasure and happiness, it won't be wasted whatever you do. This is good coffee!"

"And the eggs are just perfect, darling," said Mrs. Kane. "Daddy's right, you know; nothing that brings happiness is ever wasted. Don't forget those three camp beds will be arriving tomorrow. Farmer Leadbetter's bringing them over from the vicarage in his van."

"We won't forget the beds, Mother, and we'll make

them up, of course," Georgie promised blithely, "and we'll get some toys for the little Duponts out of that money. Something to greet them when they arrive!"

She pinned the precious note into the pocket of her shirt. As she rushed out of the bedroom, she smelt the fatal aroma of burning bacon floating up the stairs. Mr. and Mrs. Kane looked at each other and laughed.

"The five pounds is nearly spent already," said Georgie's father, "and the one person who will have none of it will be our only daughter. But she's certainly learning how to live."

Down in the kitchen Georgie was faced by a hot-cheeked, defensive Susan, and a patronizing Geraldine.

"I *like* toasted bacon," Susan was saying defiantly, "and it just so happens that I've cooked mine first!" She took the blackened wisp out of the frying pan and put it tenderly on to a plate.

"O.K.," said Georgie cheerfully. "Do mine next, will you, and then we can have ours. The others can wait till Mother and Daddy have gone."

Susan managed to look surprised, haughty, and grateful all at once, and fried the next rasher fairly well. She and Georgie sat down to eat their impromptu breakfast at the kitchen table, while Gerry wandered off. By some sleight of hand Susan succeeded in getting her uneatable bacon into a piece of paper, which she rolled up in her handkerchief, and put into her pocket when Georgie was not looking.

Everyone felt rather flat when Mr. and Mrs. Kane had gone. Georgie and Susan cooked breakfast for Gerry and the three boys, and then went to find Spot and Timbo.

The two ponies were very friendly by this time, having spent most of the summer holidays together. They were in a beautiful field which adjoined the Wychwood land, and as soon as they heard the two girls scrambling through the hedge their ears pricked up and they came trotting to meet them. Susan had ridden since she was a child and was used to riding, but Georgie had had nothing to do with horses or ponies till the previous Christmas holidays.

"He *is* the Best-tempered Pony," Georgie declared, "as they said at Whitelea."

"Yes," agreed Susan. "Still, as Gerry keeps rubbing in, it was only a tiny affair among friends. I wonder——"

"What, Sue?"

"Well," she said, "I wonder how he'd make out at a real show?"

"In open competition, you mean?" Georgie looked thoughtful. "He'd still be the Best-Tempered Pony," she reflected, "and I'm sure he'd do well in the events. Only, I couldn't ride him, could I? You—Sue! You don't mean to *take him to Stonebridge*? But it wouldn't be any good!"

Susan's jaw was squarer than usual. "Why wouldn't it?"

"Well, you said yourself that entries have to be sent in, and, and all that," Georgie ended rather feebly, her voice trailing off as she pictured a glorious scene outrivalling the Field of the Cloth of Gold.

"This is only Friday," Susan said patiently. "I'm sure there's time."

Georgie's hazel eyes grew dark with excitement. Gerry's little dig about Whitelea had rankled, and she felt a very natural desire to know how Spot would acquit himself among strangers.

"We must find out how far it is," said the temptress,

"and then perhaps we could take him over today. I'd come with you, of course, on Timbo, though the only prize *he'd* win would be the Pony-Most-Like-A-Barrel! Georgie! We could do it!"

"We're crazy! Of course we couldn't! What about tonight?" cried Georgie, and Susan waved her hand.

"It's quite fine today. We could camp out with them. Have a bivvy—something like soldiers used to! Or do I mean a barbecue?"

"No bivouacs for us, thank you. We'd freeze to death, and die of pneumonia, and probably be arrested as gipsies as well! I say, shall we have a ride now?" asked Georgie, as Spot turned his head and looked her full in the face. He had beautiful eyes, friendly and fearless, and bright with intelligence.

"Let me ride him," Susan said unexpectedly. "Just to see. If we did take him to Stonebridge——"

"But you know we can't! We can go ourselves, of course, by train or bus. But we couldn't take him over today and just dump him till tomorrow, and we can't take him tomorrow and expect him to compete after a long ride. Forget it!" Georgie advised, but without much hope. Susan was very tenacious of her own ideas, and never seemed to see when they could not be put into practice.

A sudden rustling in the hedge made them both turn. There were the twins coming to join them. Tough had a bag of small apples, as the ponies immediately guessed.

"Hallo," said Rough. "We wondered where you were, and then we saw something that was either a bonfire or Sue's hair, so we trailed it. You two look kind of gloomy. Is anything wrong?"

"No, we're just thinking," Georgie said in a tone that

was purposely vague. But Susan turned to the boys in her usual headlong fashion, and asked them if it was too late in the year to go camping.

After that, of course, Rough and Tough had to be told the whole problem, and, as Georgie had feared, they became as enthusiastic as Susan herself.

"Let us approach this systematically!" Tough said solemnly, winking at his brother. " 'First things first', as Julius Caesar said when he lit his primus stove. We've got to get a programme of this show somehow, and see what the events are, and the rules about entering."

"And the fees," Rough added prudently. "Let's go over to Driscoe now. Somebody's sure to know."

"Cox's will know," said Georgie, her scruples deserting her. "That's the big corn merchant's shop in the High Street, where they sell saddles and embrocation and mousetraps—everything! There are always notices there. As a matter of fact, I saw some yesterday when I was in there, but I didn't stop to look. Oh, Sue! Not again!"

"Sorry," said Susan, who had begun to hum *Strawberry Fair*. "I was just thinking that if we could find out about this Show, I'm perfectly certain we could do something. Let's all go to Driscoe!"

"You go with Rough and Tough; Sue and you can ride Mother's bicycle. But I'd better stay here in case those beds come. Peter is going into Exeter to meet friends for lunch, and I don't think we ought to leave Gerry all alone," said Georgie, who often suffered twinges of conscience on her cousin's behalf.

Susan said no more, but she did not go into the market town with the twins. She kept out of everyone's way, and when the ponies' field was deserted, she quietly saddled Spot and made him trot and canter, and then

Susan jumped the low post-and-rail fence which divided the field from pasture land beyond

jump the low post-and-rail fence which divided the field from pasture land beyond.

She was a most loyal friend, as Georgie knew, and she was very fond of the whole Kane family, as her own parents were abroad so much that she was left far too often in the care of her elderly Uncle James. There was nothing the warm-hearted Susan would not have done for Georgie or any of the Kanes, and her dislike of Gerry was founded on jealousy. Unfortunately, Susan was a very slapdash person, always inclined to act first and think later, and this sometimes made her friendship a doubtful blessing.

It was not until she put Spot to a gallop that it occurred to her that perhaps she ought not to be riding Georgie's pony without permission, even though she had the noblest motives in the world. Overcome by embarrassment, she pulled him up too sharply. He did not mean to throw her, and it was entirely her own fault that she went clean over his head.

She was winded, but not hurt. Thank goodness no one was watching! That was her first thought as she scrambled to her feet and began to pet Spot, who was standing some distance away looking restive and miserable.

"Cheer up!" she said. "It was me, not you, and we're both all right. But I think I'll go in and take off my frock. Gosh! What *would* Miss Primrose say if she thought I'd been riding like this?"

Guilt now overwhelmed poor Susan, and she slunk back to the house, imagining the head mistress's strictures on her behaviour and attire. Thanking her lucky stars that no one was likely to find out about either, she wriggled out of her grass-stained cotton frock rather gingerly, because the back of her neck was aching a bit.

She put on her jodhpurs and the yellow shirt she had worn the day before.

Looking as innocent as nature would permit, she found Georgie and Gerry. They were sitting in the dining-room, trying to smooth out the crumpled pages of last week's *Driscoe Echo*.

"I found it in King Toby's basket," Georgie explained; "that's why it's this funny shape. Gerry thinks it would be nice to go to Stonebridge tomorrrow, if we can get there easily."

"Are you looking for a notice about the Show?" Susan asked in some surprise. "But I thought the Lads . . ."

Georgie gave her a warning glance. "Gerry thinks she saw Stonebridge mentioned in the paper, that's all."

"Oh, here we are!" Gerry exclaimed. "Nothing interesting, I'm afraid." And she began to read aloud:

CHILD ROBBED OF PET

Little Felicity Brown (12) was not living up to her name when I saw her yesterday at her grandmother's riverside home. In fact, tears were not far away, for Felicity's pony Cherry Pie is no longer in the paddock where he has lived for so many years. He has been stolen. 'We have no idea who can have done this dastardly thing," said Mrs. Millicent Brown, when I interviewed her in her spacious drawing room. 'My grand-daughter is heartbroken, and I am appalled.'

"Don't read any more," said Susan. "I bet she goes on about this modern era, and teenagers. And I don't call a girl of twelve *little*, do you, Georgie? I think whoever wrote that was spinning it out to fill up a page, the way

I do sometimes in English. I mean to say, what has the size of the drawing-room got to do with it?"

"Poor Cherry Pie," said Georgie. "I wonder what's happened to him. Was this the paragraph you meant, Gerry?"

"Yes, the bottom bit," said Gerry. "Your precious Toby's sweet little claws have torn up the middle. Yes, this is it, Listen!

'Known as The House with the Mystery Room, Lebanon Lodge has baffled historians and architects for the last three centuries. For although seven windows may be counted along the north wall from the outside, only six appear from within.'

"I'd like to see that. It would be something different to tell the girls, when I get back to St. Monica's."

"Let's go, then," Georgie said gently. She knew that Gerry found her holidays rather dull, for she had never really settled down at Wychwood. Gerry's parents, far away in Singapore, did not seem to bother about her much, and so her real life was lived at school.

"I say!" cried Susan. "Lebanon——"

"Hi!" called Rough, as he and his twin entered the room at a gallop. "We've been hunting for you, Georgie and Sue."

"Don't mind me, will you?" Gerry said, with an acid smile.

"We don't!" said Tough, but he gave her a wide, friendly grin. "We went to Cox's, and the man we spoke to told us all about the Show, and gave us his own programme, as they are all sold out. Here it is! And there *are* some races people can enter on the spot."

"Lebanon——" said Susan.

"Let you come?" asked Rough, who had snatched the programme from his brother and was reading it eagerly, much too busy to take in what Susan was trying to say. "Yes, why not? We thought you and Georgie would both come."

"I didn't say 'Let us come!'" Susan cried angrily, turning scarlet as was her wont. "I said *Lebanon*. I've been trying for the last half hour to tell you all that *that* was the name I saw written on that bit of paper yesterday!"

CHAPTER THREE

OVER THE BRIDGE

"It's no good your keeping on saying it must be a clue. What's it a clue *of*?" Gerry demanded impatiently, when Susan had recounted her meeting with the three men outside Cox's shop. "Anyway, Lebanon could be the name of a racehorse, or they could have been making a note of the tree, the cedar of Lebanon. You can't put a clue before a mystery, Susan!"

"And it *was* nosey——" Tough began, when by a stroke of luck a diversion occurred. They all heard a heavy vehicle coming up the drive, and of course there was a rush to the dining-room window.

"It's the beds," said Georgie, "though why on earth Farmer Leadbetter's brought them in his *big* van!"

"They must be great four-posters, I suppose," Rough muttered in dismay, as he and Tough and the three girls all ran out to investigate.

Farmer Leadbetter himself was driving the van, and gave them his usual cheerful smile.

"I reckon you think I'm bringing you a couple of cart-horses for a present," he chuckled. "But my small van is out of order, and these camp beds of vicar's, they're just too awkward to go in my car. So, it has to be old Noah's Ark, see?"

"Why do you call it that, Mr. Leadbetter?" asked

Susan, as he swung himself down and began to unbolt the rear doors.

"Why, you ought to guess that, Miss Sue," he responded, laughing. "It's because I move my livestock this way. It may be old-fashioned and on the noisy side, but animals travel in it comfortable as can be. Why, Timbo, he's been to Driscoe and back, in old Noah's Ark, one time I nearly sold him and changed my mind!"

Georgie's voice squeaked with excitement, "Then it's all fitted up as a horse-box?"

"Well, yes, Tom Mayne and I, we fitted it up between us. Not very smart, but it serves its purpose. Look," said the farmer. "I takes the fittings out if I have a heavy load of anything, but three little camp beds don't take up much room . . ."

He paused to stare as Georgie and Susan clasped hands and leapt in the air.

"It's the very thing! It's fate!" crowed Georgie. "Mr. Leadbetter, could you—would you—take Spot over to Stonebridge for us? Would it take up too much of your time? And, please, could one of us travel with him? Oh, I forgot!" Her face fell. "He couldn't stay out alone all night."

"Stonebridge!" said Farmer Leadbetter, looking at her with fresh interest. "You mean you're thinking of putting him in the show, eh? Well, then, you don't have to worry, Miss Georgie. The wife's cousin's out at Stonebridge—name of Carson; took over Kingfisher Farm last year. He's got a meadow not ten minutes from the Plain, where the show's always held. I could get Spot over there for you, in a matter of half an hour, and Ned Carson will turn him out among his calves, and he'll be as happy as a grig!"

"Do you mean you'd take him now?" asked Georgie, scarcely able to believe her luck, and the good-natured man nodded.

"If Master Ralph and Master Tony would take these beds," he said, "I'll come and catch Spot now for you, and you are welcome to come along too, Miss Georgie, though it'll shake you up a bit, maybe. Yes, you too, Miss Sue! There's no call to look so downcast," he added, laughing at Susan's expression of tragic entreaty.

Rough and Tough were already carrying the camp beds into the house. Georgie and Susan were ready to drag Farmer Leadbetter to catch Spot. It was left to Gerry to ask, in a chilly tone, what was to be done about lunch?

"Lunch?" Susan spoke as if food were the least important consideration in her life. "We'll rustle up something when we get back. Perhaps you could open some tins!"

"Or," said Georgie, seeing Gerry's outraged expression, "you could come with us, Gerry, and we could buy some ham and tongue on our way home."

Gerry cast a meaning look at Noah's Ark, shuddered, and said she would stay at home and forage.

It was the work of moments for Georgie to slip a head-collar on Spot, who looked surprised and rather pleased as he was led out towards the van. But he turned and caught Georgie's sleeve in his teeth before he entered it, as much as to say "Of *course* you're coming too?"

"Of course I am, Spot," she whispered, as Farmer Leadbetter settled him in. "This is going to be fun, and a tiny little adventure as well."

"Frrh!" said Spot.

Georgie wanted to travel with him, but Farmer Leadbetter made her sit in front with Susan and himself. Gerry and the twins waved to them as they set off, and Noah's Ark trundled merrily down the road to Driscoe.

Avoiding the little town, the farmer took a long winding lane which ran parallel with the river part of the way. Georgie noticed how the country changed with every mile. Cool green water meadows replaced the rocky uplands near her home, and the pretty farms and cottages looked much tamer here.

Several times they were overtaken by lorries carrying agricultural implements or produce, and when they drew near Stonebridge Plain, as the flat grassland on the left bank of the Cara was called, the girls were amazed to see so many tents and marquees already put up.

"I believe the Show's started today!" said Susan. "Look, that notice says Refreshments! And there's Ring One, and there is the Collecting Ring. And there's a little tent where someone's taking entries."

"It isn't open, though," said Georgie. "They're only getting ready. Doesn't it look nice? Oh, there's a roundabout being put up, a real one, with dragons! And that stall over there, the stripey one, is going to sell homemade sweets!"

"It's like Strawberry Fair," grinned Susan. "I *am* glad we came. Mr. Leadbetter, do we enter Spot now?"

"I don't rightly know," was his answer. "The tent's there all right, and there's Mrs. Davis and Mrs. Brent inside it, talking to Major Mulrany, who's always one of the judges. Why not go over to them, and ask them if they're taking entries? I'll be right here, looking at this combine harvester. Jowks! It's a fine one and no error; they'll be building them with transistor radios next!"

He moved across to a huge marquee where several other farmers were gathered to admire the green and scarlet monster, which, the exhibitors promised, would save a month's work in two days. Georgie went forward rather uncertainly, with Susan at her side.

The two very trimly turned-out women were deep in conversation, and did not notice the girls approaching. Major Mulrany, who was well past middle-age though still strong and active, went hurrying off with another man to help move his car, which had got wedged in a rut.

"Quick, Georgie! *Ask* them," urged Susan, about ten yards away from Mrs. Davis and Mrs. Brent.

"I'm going to," Georgie returned, "as soon as they stop talking."

"They don't look as if they'll ever stop. You'll have to interrupt!"

"Sue, I can't, I . . ."

"Yes, you can!" Susan was adamant. "Just clear your throat and say excuse me." Then she proceeded to demonstrate.

"Err-herrrm!" she began, and got no further.

"I say, Hermione!" boomed Mrs. Brent. "Someone's got a bad cold, and it *is* a bit chilly, sitting here! What about a spot of coffee? Those idiots must have got the urn working by now!"

"Err-herrrm!" said Susan once more, as she bore down upon them. "Excuse me, but I wonder if . . ."

"There *are* a lot of sore throats about this autumn," Mrs. Davis said at the same moment. "Yes, Pam, let's go and get some coffee right away!"

And up they sprang, tall, slim, and elegant in their

riding clothes, and marched off to the tent marked Refreshments, without so much as noticing Susan or Georgie.

"Greedy things!" said Susan wrathfully. "I wonder what you can get besides coffee? A bun wouldn't be bad, or perhaps there's chocolate? Well, aren't they the *limit*, going off like that to guzzle, before we'd had a chance to speak to them! I know—we'll tackle them while they're swigging their coffee!"

"No," said Georgie. "That's what Daddy would call a sitting target! Let's wait till they come back here. The sign isn't up yet, but this is obviously the secretary's tent. Let's look round for a bit. Farmer Leadbetter's still looking at that combine. I can see his cap. Let's go down to the river."

"Ye-es," said Susan, with a backward look at the Refreshment tent. "All right. It's quite near. Oh, look, there's a man with ices! That's a good idea. They'll keep us going for a while."

Armed with a large iced lolly, she raised no more objections, and she and Georgie cut through the various tents and booths, and reached the river bank.

The Cara was at least sixty feet wide here, and was very clear in the shallows. Georgie and Susan could see trout swimming about in the sauciest manner, and the banks were beautiful with late summer flowers and rushes.

The pathway was quite well defined, and they realized that when the show was not on, the view must be glorious. The Plain was green and wide, and the trees surrounding it were tall; while on the other side of the bright river they could see the gold and silver of fields nearing harvest. Ahead of them was the old grey bridge which had given the little town its name.

"And look!" Georgie cried eagerly. "There's another bridge before you come to it. A private one! Perhaps it belongs to that big house. Yes, it goes across to the opposite bank, and there's a little green door in the wall. Let's go as far as that, shall we, and then turn back! It won't take long."

Susan agreed, but with less than her usual enthusiasm. Georgie wondered if she could be tired, but forgot about it immediately, for the tiny wooden bridge had caught her imagination.

It was so small that it could have been built by goblins, though it was designed to bear human weight. It had a kind of ladder on each bank, with one handrail only. A couple of planks, with only four supports, spanned the wide stream. She wondered how long it had stood there, and whether it would bounce as one crossed it, in the usual way of suspension bridges.

"Sue, do you think it's private?" she asked.

"It's sure to be. Let's go back," said Susan, in such a queer tone that Georgie thought perhaps the recent ice cream had been a mistake.

"Wait for me, then. I *must* go over," she said eagerly, "because I've a feeling that this old house might be Lebanon Lodge. I know there isn't time to find the mystery window now, but we could have a quick look."

"Oh? Lebanon?" Susan said, with a revival of interest. "All right, Georgie, let's go over! You go first, and if the bridge gives way, I'll life-save you!"

Georgie laughed, but she proceeded very cautiously all the same, treading as lightly as she could, and never losing her grip of the handrail. The bridge vibrated a little, but that was all. Soon she had climbed down the ladder on the far side, and was standing by the old red brick wall, with its mysterious little green door.

They were in a

She turned to look at it more closely, and heard Susan's footsteps on the bridge. They stopped quite suddenly.

"Georgie! I feel funny," Susan gasped, and Georgie, spinning round, saw that she was slumped over the handrail, in midstream.

"Hold on!" she cried, and went to meet her. This time the bridge shook quite considerably, which was a sickening sensation.

Susan did hold on, and when Georgie had inched her

garden, wild but beautiful

way to her, she was able to smile. "Sorry," she muttered. "I saw stars, and everything began to buzz. I don't like this bridge!"

"I'm not so keen on it myself, now," Georgie said, in would-be bracing tones. "Hang on to me, and we'll get off as soon as we can."

As she could not possibly step across Susan, on the narrow planks, this meant that they had to land on the far side. But Georgie, edging along with Susan's cold hand on her arm, thought it would not really matter, as they could return to the path by re-crossing the big stone bridge just ahead. It would cause further delay, of course. Even now poor Farmer Leadbetter must be wondering what had become of them, and Mrs. Davis and Mrs. Brent had surely drunk all the coffee they wanted by this time.

"Here we are, Sue," she said encouragingly. "There's just this little ladder to get down, and then—look out!"

But the warning came too late. Susan had misjudged the top rung of the ladder and had come tumbling down on top of Georgie, who fell flat on her face.

Georgie sat up, dazed and muddy, and stared in alarm at Susan, who was scrambling to her feet and looking quite white. Before she could speak, however, a third person came on the scene. The little green door opened and a girl came out. She was a very pretty girl with bronze hair curling round her startled face.

"What on earth are you two doing?" she asked in an icy tone.

"Falling down, and getting up," Susan said shortly, as her temper began to rise. Georgie thought this must be a good sign, as Sue couldn't be really ill if she could snap like that!

"Are we trespassing?" she asked, point-blank.

"No," said the girl. "People can walk on both sides of the river. But strangers don't usually fancy our bridge. It's dangerous. It might give way any minute. The river's frightfully deep here, almost bottomless, and the bank on our side is pretty boggy. You could be sucked down quite easily."

She spoke with a deadly earnestness that shocked Georgie into silence. She did not believe in bottomless

pools or hidden quagmires in a civiliz
but she did sense hostility on the part
stood in a defensive attitude, her hand
curled into fists.

"Don't worry," said Georgie. "We're g
won't come back!"

The girl flushed crimson, and her dark blue eyes shone with sudden tears as she realized how very rude she had been. "I'm sorry," she muttered, and then, as if she had noticed for the first time that they were in jodhpurs and sweaters, she asked if they were staying in Stonebridge for the Show.

"Not staying," Georgie said. "We've come from Dockleford, the other side of Driscoe. Sue—there *is* something wrong!"

She and the bronze-haired girl sprang forward just in time to save Susan from toppling over. She was now "so white that she was green," as Georgie said afterwards, and offered no resistance as they led her away from the water's edge.

"You'd better come in and lie down," the strange girl said abruptly, and with her foot she pushed open the little door and went through, pulling Susan and then Georgie after her.

It was just like walking into fairyland. If Georgie had not felt so anxious about Susan and conscience-stricken about Farmer Leadbetter, she would have enjoyed this unexpected adventure to the full. They were in a garden, wild but beautiful, with a mossy bank on one side of them much higher than their heads, and an avenue of trees stretching away towards the ancient house. Just ahead there was a glimpse of a lake, with some water lilies on it. And beyond that rose the mighty trunk of a cedar of Lebanon.

.. iis girl *was* Felicity Brown, whose pony had been ,tolen. No wonder she was feeling at odds with the world, thought Georgie, with a rush of sympathy.

There was a seat in a tumbledown arbour, under the trees. Felicity led them to this, and soon Susan was sitting down and beginning to look more like herself.

"I felt tired," she muttered, in reply to Georgie's inquiries. "And hungry," she added reproachfully. "If only I'd had that bun."

"Sue, you're awful!" Georgie protested, but Felicity took it quite seriously.

"I'll give you a bun," she said. "At least, it's cake really——" And she vanished, the brown woollen dress she was wearing merging into the mass of trees.

"She'll be ages," said Georgie. "Oh, gosh, what will poor Mr. Leadbetter think? And Spot? He'll feel we've abandoned him. Will you stay here, Sue, while I rush back to the Plain?"

"Calm down," said Susan, more cheerfully. "Here's that girl now, with fodder. She *can't* have run to the house and back! Georgie, this is a funny set-up. Do you know, I believe this *is* Lebanon!"

CHAPTER FOUR

THE GATE-CRASHERS

FELICITY, coming back to the arbour with a paper bag filled with eatables, heard the last word, and her face hardened. Georgie had purposely refrained from telling Susan not to mention the house of mystery, because Susan was not only devoid of tact, but quite unable to see why it was ever necessary at all. Felicity scowled at them both.

"Yes," she said, "this *is* Lebanon Lodge, and I *am* the girl who owns Cherry Pie. Owned him, I mean. But if you've come to see the mystery window, it's not on view!"

"We don't want to see it, thank you," Georgie said quietly. "We haven't time. As soon as Sue's better—this is Susan Walker and I'm Georgie Kane—we'll have to get back to the Plain. There's a pony waiting for us, and a farmer," she added, as an afterthought, "who'll be having fits by now!"

Felicity's pretty face was much prettier when she smiled.

"Eat this up," she said to Susan, passing her the bag, "and you'll soon feel better. You know who I am, I suppose—you must, if you read that barmy article in the *Driscoe Echo*. What's your pony like."

Georgie's face lit up. "Spot's a chestnut, and the most beautiful . . ."

"Next to Black Agnes, he's the best pony I know," said Susan, munching a piece of very dry seed-cake with some difficulty. "We've brought him over to enter him for tomorrow if we can. Do you know Mrs. Davis and Mrs. Brent?"

Felicity laughed shortly. "That's like asking someone who lives in London if they know Big Ben! Of course I know them—they always help Major Mulrany to run these shows. Besides, Judy Davis and Pat Brent go to my school." She grimaced, as if this were a distasteful subject. "If you feel all right now, Susan, I'll show you a short cut back to the Plain."

"Not that bridge again?" Susan asked in alarm.

"Oh, golly, no! It isn't *safe*," Felicity said emphatically, "and this part of the garden's rather dangerous too. I told you the bridge might give way—well, the earth here gives off a poisonous vapour, because it's so marshy. No, I'll take you out the proper way, and put you on your road. I think I must put up a notice to warn people off."

Georgie and Susan exchanged glances as they agreed that this might be a good idea. "I'll never trespass again!" Susan murmured. "This has cured me for life. I—Oh, my sainted cats! *Now* we're for it!"

Felicity had by this time led them through a shrubbery to a fairly broad grassy walk, and the two intruders were horrified to see a tall, majestic figure coming towards them. The grandmother, of course, thought Georgie, thinking of the article which seemed to have displeased Felicity so much. She fully expected the old lady to be angry, and was therefore very much surprised to be greeted with a smile.

Mrs. Brown had no trace of her grand-daughter's rather elfin beauty. One could tell at a glance that she loved the country and animals, and had probably excelled at every sport she had taken up. She had keen blue eyes that looked straight at one, and although she was fairly lame now, she was very upright.

"Good morning," she said, to Georgie and Susan, and glanced inquiringly at Felicity, who took a few seconds to realize what was expected of her.

"Oh, of course!" she said, not very amiably. "These are Georgie and—er—Susan, Grannie. Mrs. Brown, my adopted grandmother!"

Georgie and Susan felt very awkward, especially when they saw Mrs. Brown's sunburnt skin redden with embarrassment. "Why must we always get caught up in mysteries?" Georgie wondered helplessly. "We've merely brought Spot over to the Show, yet we seem to have landed bang in the middle of a strange situation."

"Felicity, that wasn't necessary," said Mrs. Brown, and to the other girls she said quite simply: "Felicity is the adopted child of my son and his wife, who died last year. But I'm wondering what you two are doing here. You're not local children, I know."

So Georgie had to tell her story yet again, though by this time she was almost dancing with impatience. Fortunately Mrs. Brown realized this.

"You must get back at once," she said. "It isn't right to keep people waiting. I'll walk along with you, I want something from the village. Are you coming, dear?" she asked Felicity.

Georgie found herself studying the younger girl's face with interest. Felicity wanted to sulk, but she also wanted to see more of the two strangers. Curiosity won.

"Might as well," she muttered, and fell into step beside Georgie.

Mrs. Brown walked quickly, despite her limp, and she took them across several fields marked Private, because she said she knew the farmer who owned them, and he wouldn't mind. The talk was naturally all about the Show, which was an annual event.

"Did you ride in it last year?" Georgie asked Felicity who nodded.

"Yes, but I was no good. Didn't win a sausage. Not that I cared, but it was tough on Grannie and Cherry Pie!"

"I wish you could have entered this year," Mrs. Brown said with a sigh. "Still, it can't be helped. Well, here's the Plain," she told Georgie and Susan, "so Felicity and I will leave you, when you've found your pony . . ."

"The van's moved!" cried Georgie. "It was under those chestnuts over there."

"I can see it," said Susan. "Look, it's much nearer now, and here's Farmer Leadbetter coming towards us. He looks grim. We're in the dog-house!"

This, however, was by no means the case. The farmer hurried up to them, full of apologies.

"I'd never have slipped off to Kingfisher Farm, and that's a fact, if I'd known it was going to take all this time," he began. "Ned Carson, he's in a proper tizzy today, and small wonder. He had a colt, you see, that was going to make their fortunes and all. Pretty little thing it must have been, if it took after its mother. Nice old girl she is, gentle as a lamb, and missing her little chap cruel . . ."

"Is he dead, then?" cried Susan, and Georgie and Mrs. Brown and Felicity all waited anxiously for his reply.

"Dead? Maybe, by this time. But he was stolen, Miss

Georgie, taken out of Nine-acre Meadow, with his mother only a few yards away . . ."

"But this is fantastic!" exclaimed Mrs. Brown. "My grand-daughter s pony was stolen last week!"

"Yes, mam," said Farmer Leadbetter. "Mr. Carson, he's my wife's cousin, told me all about that and how the police come to him confidential-like. 'You'll oblige us if you don't tell anyone about your colt,' they said, 'because the thief that took one will have taken the other, and we're lying low and watching him,' they said. But this morning they changed their tune. They haven't caught the chap, you see, and with the Show coming off, they think it's only right to warn folks about horse thieves. And Ned Carson won't hear of putting up Spot for you, Miss Georgie. He says what happens once can happen again!"

"Then we'll have to take him home," Susan said, in bitter disappointment, "and give up all hopes of the Show!"

"Rather than risk losing him!" said Georgie. "Poor little colt, I hope whoever's got him is treating him well."

"That's what Mrs. Carson is saying too. It's hard," said the farmer, "when it's the first time they've bred a strawberry roan——"

He paused in surprise as a strange sound come from Georgie. Actually she had been winded by a dig in the ribs from Susan's very solid elbow. Remembering how Susan had seen the word "Lebanon" on that scrap of paper, both the Grange girls glanced involuntarily at Felicity, who rewarded them with a stony stare.

"Of course you needn't withdraw your pony," Mrs. Brown said to Georgie. "We have good stabling at

Lebanon, and Perkins, our gardener, will look after him with pleasure."

Georgie swallowed nervously, appalled by the idea of leaving Spot in that ill-omened house. She wouldn't do it, of course, she told herself, but she must find a way of refusing gracefully.

"Thank you very much," she said. "It's terribly kind of you, Mrs. Brown. But I'd rather take him home. I don't ride much yet, you know, so he wouldn't have gone in for many events. We just brought him over on a sudden impulse, so it's much better for us to take him straight back."

"Oh, I don't know!" said Susan, giving Georgie one of her outsize winks. "It does seem a pity, when you've brought him so far. I'll ride him for you, of course, in anything you don't want to tackle. I thought you understood that."

And Susan eased the back of her neck as she spoke, thinking of that secret practice she and Spot had had together. She must have strained something to get all muzzy like that, by the river.

"If you're thinking of Cherry Pie," Mrs. Brown said to Georgie in her straightforward manner, "*he* was in the paddock when he was stolen, and that's a long way from the house. The stable where your pony will be housed is part of the kitchen wing, and no harm can possibly come to him. My son used to keep his hunters there before he went abroad."

"Well, I think it's creepy!" Felicity said suddenly, "and I don't think you ought to risk it, Georgie. As for having Perkins, Grannie, you must have forgotten how slow he's getting. He'd be no help at all!"

"But Spot wouldn't need anything," argued Susan, "if he stayed just the one night! Just a meal, and a bucket of water, and some hay! And of course *we* could come over in the evening to bed him down, couldn't we, Georgie?"

Georgie was beginning to feel like the pivot of a seesaw. Susan for some reason wished to keep in touch with Lebanon, while Felicity was equally determined to shake off her new acquaintances with all possible speed. Georgie herself naturally shrank from going where she wasn't wanted, and tried to think of a way to muzzle Susan.

Then Mrs. Brown spoke, and the matter was settled.

"Perkins may be slow, but he is perfectly capable of feeding a horse and putting it up for the night. His little cottage is nearby. Georgie, you can leave Spot with us till tomorrow, and feel quite easy about him. You agree, don't you?" she asked Farmer Leadbetter, who nodded vigorously.

"Yes, mam, that'll be best, and save me a mort of work too!" he said with a jolly laugh. "There's a couple of cows over Kingfisher Farm that are due to go to an estate up near Periton, and I half promised to take 'em!" he explained, "seeing that Ned Carson's van is in dock at present. If we don't have to take Spot home I can load the cows right away, and take 'em to their new field after I've dropped the young ladies at Dockleford."

"Goody, goody!" said Susan gleefully. "So that's settled! Georgie, let's go and enter Spot now! How much money have you got? In other words, how many races can he enter? And which ones?"

"Oh, do stop, Sue, you sound exactly like an exam paper!" Georgie protested. "I haven't studied the programme properly, though I did tick a few things off in the van coming over. 'Best-cared for Pony', and I did wonder about the Bending, and Musical Bundles."

"There's Jumping Under Fifteen," said Felicity, forgetting her antagonism for the moment. "You *are* under fifteen, aren't you?"

"Yes, I'm fourteen, but I don't jump," Georgie confessed.

"I do," Susan reminded her, for the second time that morning.

"Come with me to the tent," said Mrs. Brown, "and see if Major Mulrany will give you an open entry. You pay fifty pence now and enter your pony, and then you needn't do any more till tomorrow, when you must declare which races you wish to go in for, by ten o'clock when the Show begins. Having paid your fifty pence, you only need to pay twenty pence a race. It's a new scheme which they began last year, for the benefit of the many visitors."

"It sounds good," Georgie said slowly. "Yes, I'd like to do that, please." But she looked very thoughtful, and as she walked across the springy turf beside Mrs. Brown, she put her misgivings into words.

"These visitors, I mean, if there are so many of them, perhaps it makes it easy for the thieves. If *anyone* can pay fifty pence, and have a right to be at the Show all the time . . ."

"My dear, the police have thought of that. So have we all. And although strangers may and do enter, they all have to give some kind of guarantee. Besides," said the old lady reasonably, "the Carson colt was stolen from the farm, and Cherry Pie from his own paddock. It's shocking about that colt. I know the mother well. She is a beautiful animal, with a lovely nature. They call her Sorrel, on account of her colour."

"It's awful about Cherry Pie too," said Georgie, who

was beginning to feel a little less apprehensive about Spot's safety.

"Yes, it's so sad for Felicity, and very disappointing for the family who were going to buy him," said Mrs. Brown. "Here's the secretary's tent, my dear. I'll introduce you."

"Oh, yes—thank you! But do tell me first, was he going to be sold?" cried Georgie, in amazement. "Felicity didn't say."

"She'd outgrown him," Mrs. Brown explained, as they took their place in the little queue of people who wished to speak to the very jolly-looking Major. "He's only a child's pony, after all. I'd found him a nice home, out Truro way. Ah, now it's your turn. This won't take long."

Georgie found herself explaining matters briefly to Major Mulrany, while Mrs. Davis wrote down the particulars, and Mrs. Brent scribbled a little card, which she gave her.

"That's like a tally," she said. "Bring it to me tomorrow before ten o'clock if possible, and you'll get your number and your badge. Isn't Felicity riding, Mrs. Brown?"

"No, I'm afraid not," was the reserved answer.

"Well, it's a great pity!" Mrs. Brent said sharply. "Pat would have lent her Dimpsie, gladly."

"And Judy *begged* her to have Swallow for at least one race," capped Mrs. Davis, "but she wouldn't. You know what she is!"

"I know my own grand-daughter," Mrs. Brown said, with rather a frosty smile. "It won't do her any harm to stand down this year. Are you ready, Georgie?"

Now that she had her entry card in her hand, Georgie began to feel rather scared. Things had happened so quickly that she had not been able to sort them out, and she felt that she had been rash. Still, that part didn't matter really. Paying out fifty pence had not compelled her to ride in any of the events tomorrow; she could forgo it, at this stage, and nobody would mind. What did matter was Spot.

She turned to see what had become of Mrs. Brown, and saw her engaged in conversation with Major Mulrany. A few moments later she joined Georgie.

"Well, it's all settled," she said encouragingly. "Your pony will be taken to Lebanon at once, by one of the Major's grooms, and you and your friend will be able to go back in the farmer's van with nothing whatever to worry about!"

CHAPTER FIVE

POLICE!

KINGFISHER FARM was small and pretty, though not very flourishing. Mr. and Mrs. Carson were delighted to find that Farmer Leadbetter could move their two cows at once. They came out to talk to Georgie and Susan, and offered them lunch, but the girls said they would have it at home.

"But we'd like to see Sorrel, please," Georgie told Mrs. Carson, whose husband had gone off to find the cows.

"This way, then. Maybe it'll cheer her up to see fresh faces," said Mrs. Carson. "Proper downcast she's been ever since Shrimpy went."

"Shrimpy?" cried Georgie, in horror. "I thought he was up to show standard."

Mrs. Carson smiled resignedly, and looked towards the gate. Her four small children came tumbling in, with a basket of mushrooms, and blackberry stains round their mouths.

"We gave him a grand name," she said. "Kingfisher Gleam! But the kids, well—it's been Shrimpy from the first, and the little feller knew it. I hope he's all right, wherever he may be. Ah, we had fine plans for him!"

The children hung back at first, but soon they joined their mother as she piloted Georgie and Susan across the cobbled farmyard to the gate where the mare was standing. She was neither smart nor young, but she had a gentle face, and her unusual colour certainly made her name very appropriate. There was a wistful look about her that the girls found very pathetic.

"How long will she miss Shrimpy?" Georgie asked Mrs. Carson, who sighed.

"Quite a while yet, miss. Ah, well! What will be, will be. We were too pleased with ourselves, belike, for owning such a fine colt."

"But it was *Sorrel* who owned him!" cried the eldest child, a boy of about ten, and he put his arms round the mare's neck. "*Dad's* only lost money," he explained to her, "but *you've* lost your little horse."

"Aye, that's true enough, Frankie, though the money's not to be sneezed at!" Mrs. Carson said with a laugh as she tweaked her son's rough hair. "Well, I hear Leadbetter calling, so we'd better find him. It's past midday!"

"Is *that* all?" Susan murmured in amazement, and Georgie had the same feeling—that this morning had already lasted longer than several normal days. It was a relief to get into the bumpy van again, and both nearly fell asleep as they jogged their way back to Dockleford.

"Where's the ham and tongue?" was Gerry's greeting, and Georgie and Susan exchanged anguished looks. But Gerry only laughed.

"I knew you'd forget! It's all right. There are lots of eggs, so I can make pancakes after we've had some of the sausage rolls Auntie left us. Peter rang up. He's not coming home till evening, as those friends he's with are taking him to some quarry where Pictish remains have just been discovered."

Georgie laughed, knowing that her eldest brother would be unable to resist such a lure. But she felt a little dismayed all the same. She had been counting on his advice.

"You look a bit down in the mouth," Tough said to her later on, when they were all having lunch at last. "And you haven't told us a word about Stonebridge yet. Neither has Sue."

Susan demolished the sausage rolls with her usual speed. Her slight headache had not impaired her appetite in the least. Finally she looked up with a grin.

"You're going to say there's nothing to tell," said Rough.

"There's too much," Susan said. "That's the trouble. Why, Georgie and I haven't talked it over yet."

"No, but we must pretty soon," Georgie said, a little pucker appearing on her smooth brow. "We've told you that Spot's in a stable at a house called Lebanon. Well——"

"Wait till I've made the pancakes," Gerry said in her sensible way, "and then tell us the whole thing. I only *hope* you haven't got caught up in another so-called adventure!"

"Why *so-called*?" Susan asked belligerently, and Gerry paused on her way to the kitchen.

"Because real adventures are like stories," she said calmly. "They have a beginning, a middle, and an end. There's a house on fire——"

"Sure the pancakes aren't?" Rough murmured.

"—and you happen to be passing," Gerry continued, frowning at him, "and you see someone screaming at the window——"

"Rough would *hear* him too, I should think!" sniffed

Susan. "Or is it a muffled scream? They often have those in books."

"Rough—or anyone," said Gerry, "then covers his head with a wet cloth, rushes in, and saves the person. Perhaps they have to jump into a blanket. Anyway, people *know* about it. It gets into the papers, and in due course Rough gets a reward of some kind, and everyone knows what it's *for*! But when Georgie and Sue have adventures, they're always mysteries as well, and the papers never print them, and there's nothing to show for it. And I bet it'll be just like that this time!"

With that, she vanished into the kitchen to deal with the pancakes, and Georgie sighed.

"She's right, of course. I suppose the best adventures *are* brave deeds, but things seem to get wished on us somehow. It's not quite six hours since Mother and Daddy went off, and we've taken Spot over to Stonebridge, pledged ourselves to go to the Show tomorrow, met a very strange girl and her 'adopted grandmother'. Talked to Farmer Leadbetter's wife's cousins, and seen their strawberry roan Sorrel, and I *think* we've got mixed up with horse thieves as well!"

"Not bad," said Rough. "Not bad at all. Would you like to explain a bit more?"

"When Gerry comes," said Georgie.

"Plus pancakes," said Susan. "I'd go and help her, only——"

They all smiled, remembering that Gerry scorned help from anyone. And in any case Susan was a menace in the kitchen, as Mrs. Kane well knew.

Gerry returned presently with a large dish piled up with her handiwork. They all ate the pancakes, even the chamois leather ones, with gratitude if not with gusto. Then Rough, looking suddenly much more grown-up than usual, said: "Come on, Georgie. Let's have the horse thieves first."

"That's Sue's part," Georgie demurred. "The story begins outside Cox's shop yesterday afternoon."

So Susan, mopping up the last pancake, told them about the three men she had seen looking at the large saddle, and the joking remark one had made. She told it in full detail this time, and nobody dreamt of echoing "Nosey!" when she referred to the piece of paper she had picked up.

"Then," said this new, grown-up Rough, "you mean you've actually seen the owner of the house called Lebanon, and you didn't mention the paper? And you went to Kingfisher Farm, where a strawberry roan colt has been stolen, and you didn't tell them that those men you met had used those very words?"

"Yes," said Georgie, flushing at his tone. "That's what I do mean. It does sound crazy, I know, but things kept on happening so quickly all morning. Sue didn't feel well, and Felicity was so peculiar, that—I *just didn't think of it*!"

"I didn't either," Susan chimed in.

"Oh, you!" said Gerry. "You never do think, but Georgie ought to have done something about it. I should say it's a case for the police."

Georgie looked at her in amazement. The police! Hitherto it had been just another of the mysteries which, as the family said, she seemed fated to meet from time to time. Now it took on a new and much more sinister aspect.

"Gerry's right, Georgie," said Rough. "You ought to tell them soon."

"All right," said Georgie, "when Peter comes back."

"He may not be back for hours! You know what the

Professor's like when he's let loose among ruins and all that junk," said Tough, who was no archaeologist. "You can't wait for him. There's no need, anyway. We're here!"

"You mean you'll come with Sue and me to see Twinkletoes?" Georgie quavered. This was the nickname the Kanes had given, long ago, to the portly Dockleford policeman, who was very popular wherever he went.

"What do you think?" countered Rough. "We'll all come, the second we've finished lunch. What, Gerry? *Washing up?* That'll have to wait. Don't miss this chance of seeing Twinkletoes raising his posse and galloping to Stonebridge!"

But when lunch was over, and the three girls, two boys, and two dogs all descended upon the little police house, he lost his bravado and became as silent as the rest.

A fresh-faced woman answered Georgie's knock, and smiled at them inquiringly.

"Is Mr. Twink—Twickenham in?" asked Georgie, blushing at her slip.

"No, I'm sorry. He's had to go to Driscoe crossroads, as the traffic's so heavy, what with the show at Stonebridge and all. Can I take a message?" asked his wife.

"Yes, please!" said Georgie, snatching this chance to temporize.

"No, thank you, Mrs. Twickenham," Rough said at the same moment. "It's something we ought to report, and my sister will ring up Driscoe."

"I see," said the policeman's wife, relieved. "The number is 124, and ask for Sergeant Green."

"This show seems to be quite popular," Gerry remarked suddenly. "Yet we hadn't heard of it till yesterday. But of course we've been away, and have only just come back."

"Yes, and it *is* only the last few days it's become so publicized," said Mrs. Twickenham. "That business of that poor old pony being stolen caught people's fancy, maybe. Of course Stonebridge isn't sorry. The show's a big thing for the town, you see. Well, all I know is the traffic is alarming, added to the usual end-of-the-summer crowds!"

"I bet Twinkletoes will have a few corns before he's finished!" Tough murmured unfeelingly as the five set off down the road again. "What now? Go home, I suppose, and ring up."

"It's the simplest way," said Gerry. "I wonder you didn't do that in the first place, Georgie!"

It *might* have been simple if Sergeant Green had been in a better temper, but it so happened that earlier in the day he had reprimanded a group of children who were playing dangerously near the railway line, and as they were bored and had nothing to do, they decided to persecute him. The police station telephone was much busier than usual that day. There had been so many bogus messages that the poor man was naturally furious. Georgie's call happened to follow a particularly outrageous one, stating that the river was in flood and ten divers were required immediately.

"Is that Driscoe Police Station?" Georgie asked breathlessly, too nervous to wait for her call to be acknowledged.

"It is!" said an ominous voice, and she rushed on.

"I just wanted to tell you about some horse thieves. At least, I can't tell you much, but I think, we all think you ought to know!"

"Name and address, please!" barked the harassed sergeant, who mistook Georgie's agitated manner for suppressed laughter.

"Oh!" Georgie, like many other people, was always put off by hostility, and Sergeant Green's voice was scarcely encouraging at that moment. "Oh," said Georgie, losing her head, "I don't *know* his name or address, and I don't even know if he's a professional horse thief. I mean, he may steal other things as well."

"Now, listen, I've had enough of this!" roared the sergeant. Rough, who was standing beside Georgie, quickly pushed her aside and took her place.

"Good afternoon, sir. I'm afraid we're not explaining very well, but——" he said, and got no further.

"So it *is* you lot again!" snarled Sergeant Green. "You'll be sorry for this, my lad. We'll find you, never fear. Now you get along home and don't you ring up here again, understand? We haven't time to waste on cheeky youngsters and their tales. Horse thieves! Huh!"

Rough put down the receiver and looked round, almost as startled as Georgie herself.

"We made a hash of that," he said. "I don't believe he thought we meant it."

"Can you wonder?" asked Gerry scathingly. "Let *me* try!"

The others watched while she got the number in her usual competent manner. She held the receiver so close to her ear that they could not hear any fireworks from Driscoe, but they saw her flush to the roots of her hair before she cried out, "All *right*, then!" in a most un-Gerry-like way. She refused to tell them what the sergeant had said.

"I expect they've had so many calls about the horse thieves that they're getting fed up," said Susan, which

"Is that Driscoe Police Station?" Georgie asked breathlessly

seemed quite a sensible explanation to the others, though of course it was quite untrue.

It was tea time now, and they all realized how tired they were after this strenuous day. They spent a fairly quiet evening, and about seven o'clock Mrs. Kane telephoned from Shadow Water, to know if everything was all right.

"We're fine," Tough assured her. "How are the Duponts, Mother? Were they? Oh, yes. Why, what crazy ideas some people get. It's Georgie's turn to speak, so good-bye!"

Georgie held the purring King Toby close to the receiver and asked her mother to guess what the sound was.

"Well, I hope you'll all keep purring, darling, till we get back," laughed Mrs. Kane. "I was telling Tough just now, Mélanie and the children were so pleased to see us, and we're very glad we came. But I'm sure Mélanie's quite shocked to think of our leaving you all on your own. She said she hoped you wouldn't get up to mischief."

"Ah, but you see," Georgie said with great dignity, "she's used to dealing with small children, not reasonable and responsible people like us . . . Here's Sue, Good-bye, Mother darling!"

Mrs. Kane at last announced that she would be bankrupt if she talked any longer, and said good night to everyone. "And go to bed early!" was her parting injunction.

"And do you know," said Rough, between yawns, "I really think we will!"

"Boys!" said Susan. "Honestly! You haven't done half as much as Georgie and I have, and yet we're not—ow yow!—yawning our heads off . . ."

"Neither am I," said Gerry primly, "though housework and cooking are quite tiring in their way."

"Oh, Gerry," Georgie said in contrition, "I *am* sorry. Truly I am. We've left you all the donkey work today. But there won't be any housework tomorrow. I'll push that casserole into the oven, and Peter will look after it, and we'll just picnic and enjoy ourselves at Stonebridge. By the way, Peter ought to be home soon now. It's after eight."

"There's the phone again," said Rough. "Sergeant Green is grovelling for our forgiveness."

"Silly, he doesn't know our number," said Gerry, as she ran to answer it this time. "Yes? This is Wychwood. Oh, *no*! Well, of course it's the only thing to do. Yes, I'll tell Georgie. Oh, dear!"

CHAPTER SIX

ON THE WAY!

GEORGIE and Susan both had the same dreadful thought. Could Spot have been stolen? They fairly flew at Gerry as she replaced the receiver. "Of course not!" said Gerry. "That was the mother of Peter's friend. He's suddenly developed spots. Peter's got to stay the night, because they won't know till the morning whether it's measles or not!"

"If it is, he'll be in quarantine," said Susan tragically, "and perhaps he won't be coming home tomorrow, for fear of passing it on to us. That'll mean he won't be able to look after Toby, *or* go back to school when term starts!"

"It may not be measles," said Georgie, as cheerfully as she could, but she had a nasty blank feeling inside. She had been longing for Peter's return, to ask him what to do about the police. Common sense told her that there was a mistake somewhere. Still, it couldn't be helped now. It was certainly no good ringing up the irascible Sergeant Green again.

"Toby will be all right," she said firmly, "Peter or no Peter. We'll leave his meal ready for him. We *must* go to the Show now. We've burnt our boats."

"Watch out it isn't your fingers as well," was Gerry's grim warning, as she betook herself to bed.

Georgie, Susan, and the Lads, however, now felt quite wideawake, and had an impromptu cocoa party in the kitchen. At last they were able to study the programme of events for the morrow. The two boys were so keen that Georgie was sure they would want to take up riding themselves one day.

"Having paid that fifty pence," she said thoughtfully, "I can go in for anything for twenty pence a time, which is awfully good. Or, at least, Sue can. She's going to ride for me, you see, if it's anything complicated."

Susan simpered and bowed. "A pleasure, I'm sure!" she minced. "How many races can we run to? I'm broke!"

Poor Susan had far more pocket money than most of the Grange girls, but somehow she was always penniless. They all laughed, and Georgie nearly told them about the five pound note in the pocket of the shirt she was still wearing, and then she remembered that she had meant to spend it on a surprise. She still had another pound of her own, which would run to five races, as well as bus fares.

"Let's see," she said, poring over the pages. "Junior Jumping—that'll be for kids, I suppose. No, it says not over thirteen! That'll be all right for you, Sue. And here's one for me, Afternoon Tea Race."

"What on earth's that?" Tough wanted to know. "Do you have to drink tea as you go along?"

"Of course not," laughed Susan. "You'd choke! We've heard of this. Someone at Whitelea was talking about it. It's simple. Each rider has to have a stooge, who's waiting by a table at the other end of the ring. You ride over to your stooge, who's got two garments waiting for you, and you have to dismount and put them on, while the stooge holds your pony. Then you remount, circle the table, stop again to pour a cup of tea, which is only water really, out of a teapot into a plastic cup. Then you empty the cup, put it upside down on the saucer, and ride home."

"You call that simple?" gasped Rough, holding his hand to his head.

"But it is!" said Georgie. "It's only an exercise in mounting, dismounting, walking, trotting, and having your pony under control. No jumping. The dressing up business is only to make it look difficult."

"You can do *that* on your head," said Susan thoughtfully.

"I hope I won't!" laughed Georgie. "I'll try it then, if you'll be my stooge, Sue? I'll take my school beret, or Mother's little pink hat!"

"And you can have my blue cotton frock, the one I had on yesterday, it's nice and wide," said Susan, reflecting that it was also easy to ride in, as she had proved. "It's simply filthy," she added happily, "so you needn't mind what happens!"

"Thanks!" said Georgie. "I'll tick that one, then. And what about Musical Bundle? Will you try that?"

"No, I'll jump, Bundle's easy enough," said Susan. "You'll be O.K. there. It's just a ring, and each person is given a sack of straw to carry. There's music, of course, and when it stops——"

Everyone nodded vigorously, and Susan asked Georgie whether she could afford the Bending race as well.

"Those two will be enough for me," Georgie said, with feeling, "so you have another one. Here you are—'Best Rider under Fifteen'."

"How ever many events *are* there?" Tough asked curiously. "This show's going to last all day. Bird

Fancier's Section—that's where we'll be," he added to his brother, "and the Sheep Dog Trials . . . though we'll have to watch Spot gallop to victory, of course. Gosh, this is unusual—Parade of Veterans. It sounds like an Old Crocks Race!"

"They're not crocks at all," Georgie said defensively, "You haven't read the bit underneath. 'Open to horses and ponies of 12 years and over. To be led by owner round Ring Two, and submit to tests in obedience and good temper. Prizes,'—h'mm!—'ten pounds, five pounds, and three pounds'. Entrance fee fifty pence, though!"

"Well, Spot isn't twelve years old," said Susan, beginning to yawn.

"I was wondering about Sorrel," Georgie said soberly. "It would boost her morale if she won something, don't you think? She really does miss Shrimpy. That boy Frankie might lead her."

"He wouldn't have the fifty pence, though," said Susan. "I suppose the entrance fee must be bigger for that one, as the prizes are good. I wonder if Felicity would have put Cherry Pie in for that?"

"Was he over twelve, then?" asked Rough, who had not pieced together the whole story yet.

"He must have been over a hundred, I should think, by the way people talk about him!" Georgie answered. "That's one of the most puzzling points. Why should anyone steal such an old pony? You can understand why they'd want Shrimpy."

"Puzzle's the word," said Tough. "In fact, whenever I hear people talking about a pride of lions, or a gaggle of geese, or a charm of goldfinches—I like that one!—I shall always think of a puzzle of ponies. Come on to bed, everyone, before our heads reel any more!"

Georgie and Susan had to retire very quietly, for fear of waking Gerry, but they managed to do so, and fell asleep as soon as their heads touched their respective pillows. But when Georgie woke at dawn, as she nearly always did, her first thought was the "puzzle of ponies", which seemed to grow more confusing all the time. If only Peter had been available! He would have *made* the police listen; still it was no good thinking of that now. Even if the measles turned out to be a false alarm, he could hardly get home before nine o'clock, when they would all have to leave if they were going to get to Stonebridge by ten.

"It's no use worrying now," she thought, as she tiptoed to the window and peered out at the soft blue darkness. "It's going to be a lovely day. I'm sure, I can smell it!—and we'll jolly well enjoy it!"

She pulled on some clothes and crept down to the kitchen without disturbing the other girls. Rough and Tough, who were also early risers, joined her very soon, and the three of them got breakfast ready, and made all the numerous plans that are necessary before a long day out. She prepared the much-talked-of casserole, and wrote instructions for Peter, in case he should return. The twins put out food for Velvet, Plush, and Toby, all of whom were doomed to a very dull day.

Then Rough and Tough had their breakfast and set off for Stonebridge, having said the day before that they would like to cycle there. The house felt very quiet when they had gone, but Susan and Gerry were down before long. Susan was wearing her old breeches-of-all-work, and a most lamentable shirt. Gerry, on the other hand, looked like an advertisement in a magazine, captioned *What the Young Rider is Wearing*. She always managed to achieve that band-box appearance, and no one would have believed that she had worn these clothes many times that summer while staying at Whitelea.

"Oh, Gerry!" Georgie's conscience gave a sudden twinge, and she spoke remorsefully. "I never thought, I never asked you if *you'd* like to ride Spot this afternoon, or lead him in the Best-Cared-For Pony parade!"

One had to be careful with Gerry. She had picked up the actual rudiments of riding very quickly, but of course she lacked experience.

"No, thanks," she said now, in her cool remote way, but she seemed quite pleased to have been asked. "Have you got everything you need?" she went on crisply. "Clothes to put on in the Afternoon Tea race, money, a spare pair of gloves?"

Georgie nodded as each item was mentioned, and then rushed to the telephone. It was Peter, as she had hoped. His friend had not got measles, and there was no thought of quarantine. He was coming home in the morning as planned, and would get on with his treatise. He wished them all a good day at the show, and rang off.

"Oh, dear! I didn't tell him about Spot, or Lebanon, or the Kingfisher colt, or anything," Georgie said regretfully, "but he seemed in a hurry, and it would have taken rather a long time."

"So long that we shouldn't have caught the nine-fifteen bus," said Gerry. "We'll have to run as it is!"

"My clean shirt!" wailed Susan.

"No good now. You should have thought!" was Gerry's inexorable reply.

"If there's a Tramps Only race, you'll win on points!" Georgie jerked out light-heartedly, as she raced her disreputable friend to the bus stop, with Gerry a close and decorous third. The traffic was certainly heavy today. They saw Farmer Leadbetter pass in his old jeep, but he was going the other way, and could only wave to them.

"I must be bats," said Georgie. "I forgot to make any arrangements about getting Spot home! Remind me, both of you, to ring up the Leadbetters from Stonebridge. Oh, I wonder if Spot's been homesick?"

"We'll go and fetch him at once, won't we?" said Susan. "As soon as you've been to the tent. I wonder if Rough and Tough have done any investigating yet."

"They can hardly turn up at Lebanon Lodge and ask to hunt for the missing room," said Gerry, in her most crushing manner, but Georgie brushed that aside.

"That's the least important mystery, at the moment. Let's hope we can find a clue about Shrimpy, or Cherry Pie. I hope Felicity's feeling happier—it's awful when people are miserable on a lovely day like this."

It was a morning of pale gold and bronze, with a tang of adventure in the air that went straight to Georgie's head. It was going to be warm, too.

The bus came lumbering up, almost full. But there was room for the excited trio, who managed to tuck themselves into odd corners. Three uncouth passengers, sitting at the back of the bus, began to whisper together as if debating whether to offer their seats or not, but they made no move.

"Yobs!" Susan muttered fiercely in Georgie's ear. "They might have stood up. I do think they're—why, Georgie," she dropped her bantering tone, and spoke in a small, scared whisper. "Georgie, do you know what? *They're* the ones I saw in Driscoe on Thursday afternoon!"

CHAPTER SEVEN

THE FUN OF THE FAIR

GEORGIE was glad the bus was so full. The three men looked unpleasantly tough, and for the remainder of the journey she was wondering how to warn the authorities about them. Major Mulrany, and Mrs. Brent, Mrs. Davis, and their friends were sure to be impossible to reach.

Then as the bus stopped at the nearest point to the Plain, she felt relief flood through her being. Rough was waiting at the stop!

Georgie, Susan, and Gerry, and a good many of the other tightly-packed passengers got out, though the three suspicious-looking characters remained in their seats. Georgie grabbed her brother's arm.

"Look!" she said. "On the back seat! They're the horse thieves! I mean, the men we *think* might be."

Rough whistled. "We can't be certain, of course, but we'll let the police know, and then if they want to stop the bus they can. I'll do it——"

"Oh, yes, Rough, please! And come back and tell us. We'll be by the secretary's tent," Georgie cried to his retreating back.

"That's that!" Susan said with satisfaction. "We don't have to bother about those creatures any more. But why must we stay by the tent? We want to fetch Spot from Lebanon!"

Georgie sighed. She was just as keen as Susan to see the mysterious house, which had figured in her dreams the night before, but she knew that they *would* have to bother about those three men, quite a lot, till the police had got all the facts. Rough would be sure to come and fetch her, or perhaps he might even bring a policeman to the tent! But she hoped that wouldn't happen, as people would stare so.

"We'll go to Lebanon later," she promised, "but we can be filling in our entries and so on while we wait for Rough to come back."

Rough and Tough had intended to meet the bus together. After they had padlocked their bicycles and left them against a convenient wall, they set off towards the road which ran along two sides of the Plain. A sudden outburst of barking made them stop, and they saw that a poodle, who was being feverishing prepared for the coming Dog Show, had got one of its claws caught in its lead and was becoming quite frantic. The boys were both very good with dogs, but Tough was perhaps a shade more skilful than his brother when it came to something like this. "Job for you," Rough had said laconically. "I'll meet the bus and come back."

So Tough nodded and vaulted the wall which divided the Plain from the road, and in a very short time he was able to disentangle the claw, to the relief of poodle and the owner.

The owner was a very excitable, elderly lady. She had a row of small grey curls across her forehead, which made her look something like a poodle herself.

"You dear boy!" she gushed. "You must let me——" and to Tough's embarrassment and horror she reached for her handbag.

"Oh, no," he said quickly. "Thank you very much, but I couldn't——"

"Ah, but you must!" she exclaimed, and darted forward so quickly that she trod on her pet's tail. Matilda, as the poodle was called, was already ruffled, and now she snapped. By an error of judgement her sharp little teeth met in the wrong hand—Tough's!

He gasped with the sudden pain, but would have made light of it—after all, Matilda was young and her teeth were good, and it was not a bad bite anyway—if the old lady had not gone into hysterics.

"Oh! Matilda, how could you? But you didn't mean to did you, my petsy-wetsy! Oh, you *poor* boy, you look quite faint! Come, I'll take you to the First Aid tent."

"No—No, really, I'm perfectly all right. Please don't bother," begged Tough. He was far from looking faint, and was now the colour of a ripe tomato. "It's nothing! The dogs at home often nip us in play."

"Matilda was *not* playing," the old lady said emphatically, "and you are coming with me to get that wound dressed!"

As Tough said afterwards, there was nothing he could do except break away from her by force. As he could not very well do that, he had to submit to being led to the First Aid tent which was not far away; with blood trickling from his left hand and a chastened Matilda slinking miserably at her mistress's heels.

"What's this? What's this?" barked Major Mulrany, passing the tent just as Tough was going in. "Dog-bite, eh? Can't be too careful! You boys can't leave the animals alone, can you? Ah, well! Lie down for an hour after you've been bandaged. That's an order! Hope he didn't hurt your dog, Miss Mitton?"

The handsome, peppery major had strode away before the old lady could explain.

"Oh, dear!" she fluttered, as the brisk officials in uniform washed and dressed the strong hand which would bear the mark of Matilda's molars for some time to come. "I shall tell him what a help you were. But you *will* lie down, won't you?"

"No, thank you," said Tough, who was longing to get back to Rough and the girls; but public opinion was too strong for him. The First Aid people had made up a lovely stretcher only a short while ago, and they were longing to see it in use. Regardless of their patient's protests they made him lie down on it, covered him with a blanket, and left him with a cup of tea.

"Matilda and I must go now," cooed Miss Mitton, "but we'll be back."

Tough gave it up. He yawned twice and fell fast asleep.

All this happened very quickly, and so when Rough went tearing across to Major Mulrany with his message about the men in the bus, he had a most unexpected reception. The major having no idea that Tough was a twin, naturally thought that this was a case of flagrant disobedience.

"You?" he said angrily, as the boy came running up. "I told you to lie down for an hour. How dare you get up and go careering about, looking for more mischief? Go back to the tent immediately."

"But, sir——"

"Do as you're told, boy, or I'll have you sent out—and give orders that you shall not be re-admitted! I won't be flouted by a twopennorth of coppers! Take yourself off!"

Terrible in his rage, he pointed imperiously towards

the First Aid tent. Rough prudently withdrew, but of course he had no idea where he was supposed to go. He concluded, in his tolerant fashion, that the poor old chap was quite mad and must be humoured, so he went off in that direction, meaning to work his way round to the secretary's tent, where the three girls must be fuming.

He had just paused to get his bearings when he heard an awful uproar; growls and snarls and frightened cries, from a dog in distress, accompanied by screams from a terrified human. He was near the Dog Section, and like Tough he rushed to the rescue of the now almost distraught Matilda.

She was being attacked by an Alsatian who had slipped her collar as she was getting out of her owner's car. The owner, a big powerful man, was after her in a matter of seconds and soon had her secure again. No harm was done, except to the nerves of Matilda and Miss Mitton. Rough, who was unhurt, had snatched up the poodle in his arms, and as Greta, the Alsatian, was being led away, Matilda licked her rescuer's face with embarrassing fervour.

"Oh," cried Miss Mitton, "you *brave* boy, but why aren't you resting as you were told? And——" Her voice trailed into silence as she saw his left hand, sunburnt and a little dusky at the moment, but devoid of any toothmarks. Realization dawned.

"You——? Are there two of you? Twins? Oh, I can never thank you, or your brother—Yes, Mrs. Brent?"

The tweed-clad figure who had joined them smiled at her apologetically, and patted Matilda.

"Miss Mitton, my husband's so terribly sorry he let Greta escape just now. He says Matilda wasn't hurt, luckily. Our man's taken Greta now, so will you please join us for coffee? And Matilda, of course."

"How kind . . . how very kind!" murmured Miss Mitton. "Yes, perhaps it would settle my nerves."

"Excuse me," Rough said, "but could you tell me where my brother is? I know he was with you about half an hour ago."

"Oh—oh, dear, I'm so confused! Such a bad beginning to the day! Poor little Matilda, did ze g'eat big c'uel doggiee——"

"Miss Mitton," said Mrs. Brent, very crisply, "that coffee will be getting cold!" And over her shoulder she added to Rough: "Don't say anything more now. Come back later on!"

So Rough decided to make another attempt to find the secretary's tent. He thought perhaps Tough had already got in touch with the police, and decided to do nothing himself until he had found Georgie.

Georgie, Susan, and Gerry, however, were a long way away! They went to the tent, as they had intended, and Georgie produced the open entry, which really seemed to be an Open Sesame to all the pleasures of the Show, except refreshments. Mrs. Davis looked her up and down, and entered all the particulars in a fat notebook. Her squarely-built daughter Judy was about fourteen, and as she helped with various odd jobs she studied the other girls covertly. At last she smiled.

"Late entrants obviously don't get their names in the programme," she said. "So you'd better be earlier next year." She peered over her mother's shoulder. "Georgie Kane, *what's* your pony's name? Spot? But I thought he was that dreamy chestnut Felix Brown was leading."

"He is!" cried Georgie, her eyes widening in dismay. "At least, she's looking after him at Lebanon."

Judy Davis and her mother exchanged glances.

"She's not, you know," said Judy, laughing. "She did put him up for the night, but she brought him over this morning. She's probably looking out for you."

"Good gracious!" said Mrs. Davis, looking up from her notes. "I saw Felicity with that gorgeous thing, and I thought he must be hers. In fact, I thought she'd changed her mind and entered."

"Who—Felicity? Oh, Mummy, never!" said Judy. "She's just like a mule. Anyway, he *isn't* hers, so she couldn't. You'd better find her, Georgie. They'll be collecting soon."

Georgie, Susan, and Gerry did not discuss the situation until they had left the tent, and then they agreed that it was most peculiar of Felicity to bring Spot up here on her own.

"Cheek, I call it!" flared Susan. "It's her good luck that he's so sweet-tempered, otherwise she might have had a frightful to-do."

"It's an insult," sniffed Gerry. "It's as good as telling us that she doesn't want us at Lebanon, and I did want to see the mystery window."

"All *I* want to see is Spot," said Georgie anxiously, scanning the crowded scene. "I expect Rough and Tough have seen him, and are keeping guard."

This seemed such a likely theory that the three walked on, looking for the Lads and Spot, and at the same time wondering whether the police would seek them out to ask about the "horse thieves" in the bus. Then a voice, addressing the assembly through a loudspeaker, announced that ponies were now collecting for the first event, in Ring One.

"We'd better go there," Gerry said, in her sensible

way, "and make sure this little nuisance isn't there with Spot."

"She *is*," said Georgie. "I can see them both! Ring One is just over there on the left. Golly, she's saddled him and everything. He looks wonderful."

Felicity was in riding kit, and looking very business-like. She was holding Spot as easily as if he belonged to her, though he pricked up his ears and whinnied joyfully as soon as he saw Georgie.

"He's beautiful!" said Felicity, turning to Georgie as naturally as if they had been in the middle of a conversation. "Perkins helped me to bed him down, but I got up while it was still dark this morning, and went out to see him. I didn't ride him, though I'd have liked to. But I suddenly decided I'd bring him here myself. I hope you don't mind?"

"Well, no," said Georgie, whose annoyance was usually short-lived. "I'm glad you did, as it happens, because we're rather late. We're looking for my twin brothers, you haven't seen them, I suppose?"

"I haven't seen anyone," said the strange girl. "I brought Spot along our private way, the same way Grannie took you yesterday. I—I hadn't meant to come to the Show, actually, but it seemed silly not to. When Spot had to be taken there somehow . . ."

She frowned at Georgie as she spoke, daring her to show any sympathy or understanding. Georgie realized this, and managed to sound suitably offhand.

"Now you *are* here, could you stay for a bit and show us around? You know Sue already. This is my cousin, Gerry, and the boys must be somewhere about. You see, Felicity, we've absolutely no idea of the set-up here."

Felicity's slim figure went taut for a moment, and then she relaxed, and even smiled.

Felicity was holding Spot as easily as if he belonged to her

"O.K.," she said briefly. "If you think it will help, I can stay for an hour, I suppose. I say, ought you to be in the collecting ring?"

"I d-don't know!" said Georgie, in a fluster. "Sue, there's somebody with programmes. I believe we've left ours in the bus! Will you get one?"

"And one for me!" said Felicity. "No, I'll go——" and she darted off to waylay the boy who was passing with a pile of programmes under his arm.

"Why on earth did you ask her to stay?" Susan hissed indignantly, turning on Georgie the moment they were alone. "You know she's odd. We said so yesterday."

"Yes, but don't you see, she feels so miserable about Cherry Pie that she flatly refused to come to the show at all. Now she wants to, and this is the only way she can stay without eating her words. She *is* strange, but she's all right. Spot likes her, anyway!"

"Spot! He's as soft as you are!" Gerry interposed, in withering tones. "You both think people are all right, unless you see them blowing up a bank, or something. Oh, well, we must make the best of it. She's coming back."

"That was Terry Mulrany," Felicity told them, as she joined them again, and handing the three girls a programme each. "He's not bad, as boys go. I told him to look out for twins, and tell them to come to you here. You'll be in Ring One all the time. Ring Two is for the dog trials and cattle judging."

The first event had begun. It was a simple one, Trotting, 10 years and under. The small ponies and their riders were enchanting, and normally Georgie would have loved watching them. Now, however, she felt very cold and had the unpleasant sensation of having recently swallowed a prickly hedgehog. This was because the programme had confirmed her fears that the second event was to be Musical Bundles.

Susan, Gerry, and Felicity went with her to the collecting ring, and spoke cheerfully to Spot, who was looking happy and excited, unlike his rider who had grown very pale. Georgie's number was 124. "It ought to bring you luck," said Susan brightly, "as it's the phone number of the Driscoe police!"

"Oh, Sue!" A wan smile passed over the victim's face. "I don't think that did bring us luck. I certainly don't want to have any more dealings with Sergeant Green!"

"Why not?" asked Felicity.

"Well, because——" Georgie stopped abruptly, remembering that Lebanon figured in the mystery of the men they called the horse thieves. It was no good telling Felicity half the story, and there wasn't time to go into it properly now.

The loudspeaker announced the name of the winner of the Trotting race. Then a beaming eight-year-old rode out of the ring amidst hearty clapping from the spectators. Georgie saw, with alarm, there were far more than one would have expected. Just for an instant her nerve nearly failed her, and then she remembered the Grange and all she had learnt there, and told herself to keep calm. She owed that to Spot!

"Will the competitors for the next race——" began The Voice, and Georgie found herself in line with fourteen other riders, first walking, and then trotting into the ring before halting to hear the instructions.

The bundles were waiting for them. Walking, to the tune of *Men of Harlech*, they had to bend and pick them up, and then trot, to *Colonel Bogey*, till the music stopped. The second part of the race, where the competitors cantered to *The British Grenadiers*, did not concern Georgie, for she was eliminated in the trotting stage. Still, she wasn't the first one out.

"Fifth's jolly *good*," said Susan, coming up to her as she left the ring. "I wish the Lads had seen you. Where can they be? Oh, look, this is exciting!" Only two people were left in—Pat Brent and Judy Davis.

Georgie had meant to dismount, but now she was so interested that she stayed in the saddle like most of the other competitors who had retired from the race. She felt suddenly very much more confident. It was such a lovely golden day, and everyone seemed happy, and the horses looked so beautiful that one wanted to shout and sing.

Once again the music stopped. Judy dropped her bundle a split second before Pat dropped hers, and a storm of clapping began.

"This is really super!" cried Gerry. *Gerry* of all people, who so seldom approved of anything! And then, as Georgie turned towards her with a smile, her voice changed, and took on its familiar carping tone.

"Goodness, what a weird specimen! And that grubby little boy. They don't fit in at all, do they?"

Georgie swung Spot round, and saw the skinny form of Frankie Carson, with Sorrel on a leading rein.

CHAPTER EIGHT

SURPRISE ITEM

SORREL and her grim little escort certainly did strike a jarring note, and Gerry was not the only person who regarded them with disfavour. But Susan went forward to greet them, and Gerry consented to hold Spot while Georgie dismounted and felt in her pocket for a piece of sugar to offer the pretty but bewildered-looking mare.

"Hallo," said Susan, "how did you get here, Frankie?"

"Frough the gate," he responded, without the slightest intention of being rude, "same as everyone else. I paid for myself. Dad let me keep the mushroom money this year, because I'm saving up for a 'cyclopaedia. I mean, I was . . ." He caught sight of Spot, and gasped. "Cor! That's what I'd call snazzy!"

Sorrel meanwhile had cheered up considerably at the sight of the sugar, which she crunched noisily while quite a number of people looked on.

"What are you going to enter her for?" Georgie asked Frankie, as he stood patting Spot.

"Dunno, really. I thought she'd like to come. I saw people unloading, and the horses seemed to like it. And I can always go to the lib'ry and look up things in the 'cyclopaedia there."

Georgie saw that he was nervous, and probably a little worried about his family's reaction to the fate of the mushroom money. There were several encyclopaedias at home. One could, no doubt, be dispatched to Kingfisher Farm, but that wouldn't help Frankie or Sorrel now. She could hear murmurs from the crowd: "Naughty little boy, I'm sure his father can't know." "He might at least have wiped her down with a damp cloth!" And, in disapproving tones from Felicity: "I know you can stick on her back in your Nine-acre Meadow, because I've seen you, but they want a high standard here!"

"I know *that*," the boy said scornfully. "I thought maybe the Best-Cared-For Pony. We're all set on Sorrel —even Mum, and she's not one for animals."

Georgie and Susan looked at the rough mane and muddy body, and the swishing tail which had some burrs in it, and their hearts failed them. The boy had returned to Sorrel now, and had his arm round her big unwieldy halter. He was a plain child and not exactly glowing with cleanliness himself, but the love and trust in his eyes made it impossible to explain what "cared-for" meant, in this case. Georgie had an inspiration.

"Sorrel can't enter for that. She's not a pony, she's a horse! Why, she's 15 hands, at least, so of course you can't ride her. What about the Veterans' Parade?"

"Nope!" Frankie said briefly. "She had the vet once when she'd got the colic, and she didn't fancy him."

Some people tittered. Georgie was glad that Felicity was not one of them.

"The entrance fee's pretty stiff, anyway," someone said, and Frankie looked dogged.

"That'd be O.K. I've still got twenty-four pence from my mushroom money."

There was some junior jumping going on now, and the girls' attention was diverted from Frankie Carson and his problems. There were only very small, easily portable "gates" for this event, which did not last long as there were so few entrants. "It's sure to be a different story for the next jumping event," someone murmured. "Thirteen and under. They made it a really tough course last year!"

Susan glanced at Georgie with a grin that wavered slightly. Usually she loved a challenge of this kind, but her neck was still aching a little and she was not feeling her best. Georgie noticed for the first time how very shabby and dirty she looked. Of course, she was wearing that dreadful old shirt, and her hair couldn't have been combed that morning.

"Sue, you look a little windswept," she said delicately. "I'm sure Gerry and Felicity will look after Spot if we dash off to the wash-tent and tidy you up. But you'll stay here, won't you?" she added, to her cousin. "Rough and Tough are *bound* to come soon."

"Of course. Don't worry," Gerry said, "but don't get lost, or caught up in anything, will you? Where's that kid, by the way, with the old farm horse?"

"Frankie and Sorrel are watching the jumping," Georgie answered quietly, "not so very far away, so don't let him hear. No, we won't get lost; we'll be back in a tick."

The wash-tent was a very primitive affair, rigged up behind the Mouse Fanciers' Exhibition. Georgie would have liked to linger here, as she was rather fond of mice, but time was precious. She merely satisfied herself that the Lads were not mouse-fancying, and then she rushed Susan into the wash-tent.

"You must take off that revolting shirt," she said

firmly, "and have mine, which I don't need under this pullover. It looks as if you'd mopped the floor with it!"

"Well, not the floor," said Susan, as she obediently peeled off the crumpled object which had once been a pale lemon colour. "But I did knock over a vase when I was playing my recorder, and I didn't want to get it wet, so I had to wipe the table with something, and it just so happened your paint-box was there as well."

"Give me that palette rag, then," Georgie said, "and put on this one. It's not terribly clean, but it will do. Now your hair, that's it. Oh, Sue, you haven't lost your gloves? Well, nip back quickly, then, and borrow Gerry's."

It was just as well they did hurry. The junior jumping was over, and a party of volunteers could be seen preparing the ring for the next event.

"All set, Susan?" asked Gerry. "No panic, but you'd better get over to the others in the collecting ring. Georgie, Rough, and Tough did come. They rushed up like maniacs to know if we were all right. They'd been trying to find us, apparently, and Rough said he'd spoken to the policeman at the gate who'd said this was the one place where horse thieves wouldn't have a chance, and not to worry till afterwards. So they've gone to get something to eat, for all of us. They're bringing a tray."

Georgie remembered afterwards that she *had* thought it strange that Susan, mounted again by this time and ready to move away, had shown no interest whatsoever in the prospect of a snack. There was so much going on, however, that she forgot about it at once.

"Junior Jumping Number Two!" boomed the loudspeaker. "For competitors not over thirteen. Come along, please. Line up. Spread out . . . Now!"

There were twenty-four competitors this time. Quietly they filed into a straight line before the stand, and received their instructions. Pat and Judy were in for this race as well. Pat's Dimpsie was a pretty little grey, and Judy's Swallow was well-named, being a very evenly marked piebald who looked as if he was wearing a black cutaway coat.

"It's not because he's yours," Felicity said suddenly, "but Spot's the best-looking pony of that little lot. But Susan hasn't a very good seat, has she?"

"What?" cried Georgie, in amazement. Susan, who had ridden all her life, was one of those people who seem part of their mount. But Felicity was right. This morning Susan looked awkward and ill-at-ease, and they saw her put her head back for a second as if to ease a crick in her neck.

Then the twenty-four ponies trotted out of the ring, to jump in turn. As usual, there were more girls than boys riding today.

"Judith Davis," said the loudspeaker, "on Swallow!" and out came the pleasant-faced squarely-built girl on her endearing pony. There were nine jumps, starting off with a brushwood one of about three feet six. Then came a white-painted gate, then an artificial hedge, and then a red sloping one that looked like a roof.

Swallow baulked at this, but cleared it the second time. He sent a pole flying later on, but galloped off at last with only four faults. The next girl had ten faults, and the boy who followed her had eight. Now came Terry Mulrany, great-nephew of the irascible major, who rode a lively Connemara pony. He had four faults. Then Georgie, Gerry, and Felicity held their breath.

"Number 130!" announced the loudspeaker. "Susan Walker on Spot."

Susan, instead of going on to the roof-jump, reined in,

Susan was not riding well. She was holding Spot in too closely, and her body looked curiously tense. Spot didn't look as happy as usual.

"Hope they'll be all right," Gerry muttered, as pony and rider approached the brushwood jump.

"They've got to be," Georgie whispered fiercely, and greatly to their own surprise the two cousins clasped hands.

A murmur of relief rippled through the spectators as Spot cleared the brushwood beautifully, with plenty to spare. Susan seemed more confident now, and they

and turned Spot towards the clear run of the exit

fairly flew over the white gate. Then came the hedge. Susan misjudged her distance over that, and would not let Spot go until it was almost too late. Almost, not quite! He cleared it with a bounding grace, which again drew an exclamation from the crowd.

"I don't understand it," Georgie said to Gerry, in an anxious undertone. "It's not *like* Sue."

"Neither is this," Gerry said grimly, as Susan, instead of going on to the roof-jump, reined in, turning Spot towards the clear run of the exit, and quietly slid off his back!

"Keep back! Keep back, please!" commanded the two judges, as the startled crowds began to scramble under the ropes. Georgie, watching as in a trance, saw one of the stewards catch Spot, who seemed quite unperturbed, while First Aid men ran forward with a stretcher . . .

Georgie and Gerry dived under the ropes, feeling that they at least had a right to do so. But they were turned back just the same. "As if we were mere civilians!" Georgie said indignantly.

"Attention!" said the loudspeaker, and a hush fell at once. "Susan Walker, the last competitor, is unhurt. Susan is perfectly all right and resting in the First Aid tent. Will her friends, Georgie, Ralph, and Tony Kane go to her there? Will Georgie, Ralph, and Tony——"

"Come on, Gerry," said Georgie, but Gerry hung back.

"You go. The Lads will be there already. Trust Sue to make an exhibition of herself one way or another!"

"You can't fool me, you know," Georgie told her, in exasperation. "Not any more. You were just as scared as the rest of us. See what's happened to Spot, will you, and then join us."

Susan looked smaller and younger than usual, lying flat on the stretcher at the back of the First Aid tent. The boys had found her already. Tough was telling her about his enforced rest on the very same stretcher, when Georgie arrived. A tall man, obviously a doctor, was stirring something into a tumbler of water.

"There you are, young lady, that will help your headache," he remarked, "and another time you have a tumble like yesterday's, just take it easy afterwards. You're her friend, are you?" he asked Georgie. "And you didn't know she'd fallen off your pony yesterday?

She has behaved in a very foolish, wrong manner. She has some nasty bruises, but she might have had concussion. She must lie down for the rest of the day."

"Oh, please," said Susan plaintively. "It's suffocating in here!"

"Never mind, Sue, we'll think of something——" Georgie was saying, when a new figure marched into the tent. It was Felicity's grandmother.

"Good morning, Dr. Cleeve," she said briskly. "This child Susan— Ah, there she is! I'm glad you're not injured, my dear. My car's outside the gates," she told the doctor. "I believe she's staying in Dockleford. It would be no trouble for me to drive her there."

"That's very kind of you, Mrs. Brown, but she's very narrowly missed concussion owing to a fall yesterday, if you please! These youngsters!" said the doctor, and he and Mrs. Brown heaved identical sighs. "I suppose," he went on, "you wouldn't put her up at Lebanon for the rest of the day? She must be kept quiet before attempting to travel, even by car."

"Of course I can put her up. She can stay the night, if it comes to that. But how can I get in touch with her people?" Mrs. Brown asked Georgie, who had to explain that this would be quite impossible.

"That's certainly a solution," said the doctor. "It *is* stuffy in here; and besides, she's only a malingerer and doesn't deserve a stretcher. My car's actually in the grounds, so do you think we could run her over to Lebanon now?"

Mrs. Brown agreed. Susan thanked her politely, and then looked at Georgie.

"Spot's all right," she said rapidly. "He didn't refuse that roof-arrangement. I did."

"I know," said Georgie. "Thanks, Sue. You might have taken a toss, pulling him up like that."

"I had to. I was giddy, and I was afraid I'd hurt him. When is the Afternoon Tea race?"

"Soon, I suppose," said Georgie vaguely. "Lads, what happened to the tray of elevenses you were going to bring us?"

The boys exchanged guilty glances.

"I think we just left it somewhere, to watch Sue jump," said Tough. "Yes, by the Dog Department. I bet Matilda's had it by now." And he and Rough began to chuckle.

"Well, off you go now," said the doctor, "all of you. Mrs. Brown will take excellent care of Susan, and no doubt she will let one of you call at the house before you leave for home. Good luck, all of you, and no more candidates for the stretcher among you! Does the hand feel quite comfortable, Tony?"

"Yes, thank you, sir. 'Bye, Sue, be seeing you! Oh, here's Gerry," said Tough, as the familiar impeccable figure appeared at the tent flap.

"Georgie! Is Georgie here?" panted Gerry, showing signs of agitation for once. "Well, come on. It's Afternoon Tea next. Felicity's holding Spot for you, and I suppose I'll have to be your stooge!"

CHAPTER NINE

TO MAKE AMENDS

FELICITY BROWN was more than a year younger than Georgie and Susan, but she was far more experienced in the ways of gymkhanas and horse shows. So, as well as holding Spot, and walking him about a little to keep him amused; she had sent a message by Terry Mulrany to the Major himself, explaining the change of stooge, though she did not know Gerry's full name.

When Georgie and Gerry reached the collecting ring, therefore, they found everything in order. Georgie's haversack, even, was waiting for her, which was more than she deserved. She had dropped it when Susan fell, and Felicity had retrieved it and hung it on her own shoulder.

"I say, thanks! You've been a nugget!" Georgie said fervently, as she patted Spot's silken neck. "I'd have been sunk without the haversack. It's got my change of clothes in it!" And she brought out the fussy little hat which her mother had once bought against her better judgment, and the crumpled blue cotton frock which belonged to Susan. Her face grew sober as she looked at it. Only yesterday morning Susan had been wearing that frock, never dreaming of the near-accident which might have had such serious consequences.

"Good luck," Felicity said, in a much more friendly

tone than usual. "I won a fancy dress race two years ago, with Cherry Pie. I wore Daddy's pith helmet and Mummy's gaudiest overall. It did look funny!" She smiled at the recollection, and then her face clouded. "We didn't live down here then," she finished. "We were only staying with Grannie. By the way, she's turned up at the Show, so Terry told me. Warn me if you see her, won't you?"

Georgie took Spot's reins from this extraordinary girl.

"Why?" she asked bluntly.

"Why? Because I don't want to run into her, of course!" The hard expression had returned to Felicity's face. "I know what she's come for. She guessed I was here, so she followed. She hoped she'd catch me riding someone else's pony, because then she wouldn't feel so bad about Cherry Pie!"

Georgie looked at her in perplexity. "I don't understand," she said, "and there isn't time to talk now. But it sounds horrible, the way you talk about your grannie, as if she's an enemy. I think she's jolly kind."

"You saw her yesterday for ten minutes."

"And this morning. Just now. In the First Aid tent. She came to see Sue, and she's taken her back to Lebanon to rest!"

Felicity said nothing. Her eyes grew dark with anger. In silence she relinquished Spot, and walked away. Georgie turned to Gerry.

"She's made it plain enough that she doesn't want anyone at Lebanon," she said. "I don't know what harm she imagines Sue can do."

"Never mind her now," Gerry broke in anxiously. "I'm sure it's nearly time for us to start. Yes! There's the signal! Quick, give me your clothes! I mustn't lose the other stooges!"

Owing to a shortage of tables the Afternoon Tea race had to be run in heats. There were over thirty entrants and only ten could compete at a time. Georgie and Spot had to wait till the fourth, and last, heat before their number was called, which was a severe ordeal. Georgie watched from behind the ropes as the others rode up to the tables, changed clothes, and poured out their imaginary tea. She could see Gerry at the far end of the ring, waiting with the other stooges. But she was so nervous by this time that the faces of the spectators in general were just a formless blur.

Pat Brent won the first heat on her rather slow Dimpsie. Surely Spot could do better, or at least as well?

"I say, I like your chestnut," said a friendly voice beside her, and she saw that Terry Mulrany had come up, on his strongly-built Eileen Aroon.

"D-d-do you?" faltered Georgie, who was beginning to shiver. "His name's Spot."

"I know. Your brothers told me. I met them just now, by the First Aid tent. Sorry about your friend. Was she stooging for you?"

"She was going to, but my cousin's doing it now."

"O.K.," said Terry. "Uncle's gardener's doing it for me. I wanted Felix to, but she wouldn't. Listen! This is us."

There were only six riders in the last heat, but all ten tables were left in position, to make it fair. Georgie, ice-cold with nervousness, rode calmly enough to the white starting line, and glanced quickly at her rivals. Terry was only eleven cr twelve, but he was obviously experienced, and Eileen Aroon looked very formidable.

There was one other boy, a weedy person who looked almost grown up, and the rest were girls. One was Judy Davis, on Swallow.

Georgie had never cherished the slightest hope of winning this race; all she wanted was to keep up reasonably well, and not be last. Spot, however, was in excellent form that day. When the race began, he entered into it thoroughly and to her amazement and joy they reached the lined-up tables long before Eileen Aroon. Gerry was white, but game. She helped Georgie to change, with that efficiency which had often seemed so annoying, though it was a blessing now.

"Take your time," she said calmly, amidst all the bustle. "You're all right. Don't rush."

And Georgie *was* all right. She did everything that was required of her, and remounted with perfect ease, clad in her mother's hat and Susan's blue frock. She could hear the Lads' voices close at hand . . . "Come on, Georgie! You'll do it."

Yes, she'd do it—she was well ahead! She *must* do it! But the frock was flapping somehow. Spot wouldn't like it, she thought disjointedly, and gave it a sudden hard tug. By sheer bad luck she ripped off the pocket, and something small and hard sailed out of it, into the air, and landed, where? She did not know until much later that it had struck Sorrel smartly on a tender spot behind her ear. All she knew now was that there was a sudden commotion behind the ropes, and Spot's forelegs went up in the air. And the thunder of hoofs behind her warned her to get out of the way.

Spot was not out of control. She could still win the race with luck; but that would be risky for those behind her, who would have to rein in till they saw where she was going. Risky for Spot, as well. She knew quite suddenly what she must do.

She collected Spot and urged him onward, but not towards the winning line. Bearing right, she cantered off the field and into the rough part of the Plain, where she pulled up just in time to hear the cheers that greeted Terry Mulrany as he won.

"Oh, Spot!" Tears rose to her eyes, but she blinked them back. "I'm sorry, darling," she whispered. "You ought to have won that, but I frightened you somehow. Never mind. There'll be other times."

She had even managed a smile by the time she came back to the collecting ring, for she had travelled round in a circle. Gerry was waiting for her, standing with folded arms like the pictures of Napoleon.

"Must you carry burnt bacon about in your pocket?" she asked scathingly. "That old farm horse got it behind the ear, so someone said, and nearly stampeded. That's what all the fuss was about! And it seems it was a horrid burnt rasher, all sharp and brittle, wrapped up in a handkerchief. And *then*, as if that wasn't bad enough, you have to lose your bearings and bolt right out of the ring!"

"Oh, Oh, how awful," Georgie stammered. She dismounted and tried to find a hiding place from all the curious glances. She realized now how the bacon had come to be in the pocket: she had seen Susan thrust it there at breakfast yesterday! What an unnecessary thing to happen—what a *silly* trick of fate.

"Attention, please! Special announcement!" said the loud speaker. "The winner of the Afternoon Tea Race was Terry Mulrany, on Eileen Aroon, and Judith Davis was second, on Swallow. Number 124, Georgie Kane, has been disqualified, but she is highly commended for having shown consideration and resource. Will spectators kindly refrain from causing any further disturbances? It is unfair, I repeat unfair, to the competitors."

Georgie blinked. She couldn't believe it. All those coldly curious stares were turning into smiles! Several complete strangers came up to her and said what bad luck she'd had, and could they pat Spot, or give him a biscuit? And Gerry said, rather unwillingly, that although the damage was done Georgie had certainly made amends.

"Oh, Gerry, that's just what I haven't done, but I'm going to," Georgie said in a low, distressed voice, as she looked over her shoulder. "There's that poor little Carson kid leading Sorrel away, and I believe he's been crying. Will you hold Spot? I *must* talk to him!"

Rough and Tough came pounding up, just as Georgie darted away.

"Hi, Gerry, where's Georgie?" they cried. "She's wanted in the secretary's tent, Major Mulrany's got a box of chocolates for her."

"She was here a moment ago," said Gerry, "but now she's rushed off to talk to that Carson boy. You can see them together. You'll just be able to catch her before they go out of sight."

But the twins made no move to follow their sister, and Gerry stared at them blankly.

"Better leave her alone," said Rough.

"She knows what she's doing," Tough agreed. "I wonder if we can find *any* traces of that sumptuous meal we purchased about an hour ago, and lost?"

Needless to say, they couldn't!

Frankie Carson refused to speak to Georgie at first. He ducked his head, and plodded along beside Sorrel, making for the main exit. But Georgie persevered.

"You know I didn't mean to scare her, Frankie. It scared me too," she said, "and my pony. Don't go home yet. Let's put Sorrel into the Veterans' Parade I told you about. She won't mind it, truly, and I want to pay her entrance fee for that, to make up to her for that bacon."

"It's no use," said Frankie. "They don't like Sorrel. She won't never get a prize. My dad said she wouldn't. He wouldn't pay for me to come. That's why I used the mushroom money." His small snub nose turned bright red.

"Now look," Georgie said in a hurry. "I've got plenty of money today. It's lunch-time now, and nothing interesting will happen till two o'clock. The Veterans' Parade won't be till three. You take Sorrel home and groom her, Frankie, and I'll get her entry fixed up in the meantime. Then bring her back, and why not bring some of your brothers and sisters too? When the Parade is over, I'll look after Sorrel for you while you all go on the roundabouts."

He looked at her suspiciously. "No kidding?"

"Don't be silly. Why should I bother to kid you? Now go along, because you've a lot to do. You must make Sorrel look her very best. Oh, and tell your mother you're coming back. You know who I am, don't you?" she asked, as a final precaution.

" 'Course I do," was his prompt reply. "You're Miss Spot!"

She let that go, and patted Sorrel, who gave her one of those unexpectedly humorous looks which elderly horses do give sometimes.

"Good-bye for now, Frankie. It's a promise," she said, and turned away, glowing. How lovely it was to have five pounds of one's very own, to make people happy.

She stopped short, sick with dismay. It *would* have been lovely, if that crisp five pound note hadn't been pinned to the shirt Susan was wearing . . .

"Oh, no!" said Gerry, when she heard about this fresh complication. "No! I can't bear it. If only you'd taken it out of the pocket before you gave the shirt to Sue. Well, you can't get it now. Even you can't march into Lebanon Lodge after we've been practically warned off the premises, and demand to see Sue! We must have a whip round. I've got thirty-seven pence."

"I've got eleven," said Rough.

"Four and a half," Tough said sadly.

"I've got five pence," Georgie murmured. With closed eyes and an expression of agony on her face, she began to add up. "Fifty-seven and a half pence!" she said in triumph. "Just enough for Sorrel's entrance fee, so let's fix that right away, before Mrs. Brent and Mrs. Davis go for lunch."

"Leaving the seven and a half for our own lunch, I suppose!" said Gerry. "What will we do, buy a bun and cut it into four?"

"Let's get Terry to ask his uncle to let us have a meal on tick," Rough said hungrily. "We can send the money on Monday."

"No," said Georgie, "because I've got to have that five pounds. Major Mulrany might let us have the meal, though I don't think he'd be pleased. But he wouldn't pay for masses of little Carsons to go on roundabouts and have tea! So you see I'll have to go to Lebanon. I'm not frightened!" she said stoutly. "They can't put me in a dungeon, after all!"

"Can't they?" said Gerry. "I'm not so sure. Anyway, we'll soon find out. Yes, of course I'm coming too! It's my only chance to see the mystery window."

CHAPTER TEN

THE SECRET

"WE mustn't stay long," panted Georgie, as she and Gerry ran off the Plain and took the path by the river. "Rough and Tough looked so hungry! I only hope they'll last out."

"We certainly won't linger at Lebanon," Gerry answered drily, "if your friend Felicity has any say in the matter! No, we'll just get that five pound note and scram. I'm quite ready for lunch myself, aren't you?"

"Let's cross this little plank bridge, then," Georgie said, "and go into the garden by that green gate in the wall on the opposite bank. That's where Sue and I went yesterday." And she remembered how Susan had almost fainted on the bridge. "Why didn't I guess she was hurt?" she asked herself blankly. "Fancy her trying to jump, feeling like that. This doesn't seem to be Spot's day out. He might have won that jumping, and I ought to have got him home in the Afternoon Tea race. Still, he's got *one* rosette to take back to school!"

She and Gerry had crossed the bridge by this time, and were now at the small green door.

"You're sure it's all right?" Gerry asked doubtfully. "We don't want to be had up for trespassing, as well as everything else!"

"No, we're not trespassing," Georgie said. "I asked Felicity that. It's lovely inside——"

Gerry gasped when she saw that beautiful old garden. She clambered up the high moss-grown bank and stood looking up the avenue of trees which had been saplings in the days of the Tudor Queen. She saw the house, old and grey and formidable, and beyond that the ruins of Stonebridge castle; where, she vaguely remembered, a handful of King Charles's men had once held out for a week against the Roundheads.

Georgie waited for her. Although they were in such a hurry it was good to see Gerry really interested for once. It certainly was a wonderful place.

A strange noise close at hand made her jump. Gerry heard it too, for she fairly sprang down the bank and looked at Georgie with dilated eyes.

"Did you hear it? That rumbling! It was just underneath me! I believe there's going to be an earthquake! Listen, there it is again!"

And even as she spoke there came a sound extraordinarily like a door closing, and suddenly Felicity was standing before them. But what a changed Felicity! She had taken off her riding clothes and was in jeans, which were absolutely filthy. They were covered with mud and cobwebs and torn in places. And, what was still more alarming, she was shaking with sobs.

"Oh, what's happened?" gasped Georgie, running forward. Felicity, showing no surprise at their presence, just leaned against the bank and cried.

"Pull yourself together!" said Gerry in her firmest tone, but Felicity went on crying. They could see her tears making little trickles on the moss.

"Felicity—Felix," said Georgie, "try to tell us. We're friends. We're on your side."

Felicity gasped, and looked at her for a moment with drowned blue eyes.

"You won't be, when you know! He's gone, *really* gone now. He's dead—he must be, and I've killed him!"

This time she didn't cry, but stood by the bank doing nothing, her tear-stained face grey with fear.

"I'll go to the house and get someone to come——" began Gerry, but Felicity turned her head sharply.

"No, please don't," she said brokenly. "I want to have one more look." She drew her sleeve across her eyes, and began to walk up the path.

Suddenly Georgie knew what she must do. Felicity, spoilt and hostile as she seemed, was really only twelve, and in this mood of despair no one could gauge what dangers she might fall into. What had she said? "He's dead . . . and I've killed him . . ."

"Gerry, listen," Georgie said quietly. "You go to the house and ask for Sue's shirt, if you can't see her, and get the money and go back to the Show. Have a decent lunch, and tell the Lads I'll come when I can. If I'm not there by three——"

"Stop!" said Gerry. "You're making my head spin. I'll get the money, of course, and I'll take it to the Lads, and tell them to carry on with the arrangements if we're *both* not there by three. I mean," she added hastily, for she couldn't bear to use bad grammar even at a time like this, "if neither of us is there to see that Sorrel gets into the Parade. That's what you meant, isn't it?"

Georgie nodded. "You mean, you're coming back?"

"What do you think?" said Gerry. "Now, Felicity—Felix—or whatever your name is, just you relax and calm down, and tell Georgie about it. After all, if he's dead, he's dead, and it's no good having one more look!"

So saying, she sped up the avenue toward the house, tall, graceful, and slender, her jodhpurs still uncreased.

"She's right, you know," Georgie said to the dazed girl at her side. "Let's go and sit in that arbour where you took Susan yesterday, and then you can tell me if you want to. Is it—is it Cherry Pie who's dead?"

"He must be!" said Felicity. Her voice still quavered, but she had recovered sufficiently to feel for a handkerchief.

"Then you don't know?" asked Georgie, becoming more and more bewildered. She could hear running, and now saw Gerry on her way back. That transaction hadn't taken long!

Gerry came up to them, pausing for a second by the arbour to say that fortune had favoured them at last.

"Wasn't it lucky? Sue's lying on a sofa by an open window! We saw each other at once, and there was no one else about, so she gave me the note, it's in *my* pocket now; and these sandwiches which she said Mrs. Brown had just given her. You eat them now, and leave one for me!"

She handed Georgie the little pile of sandwiches, which Susan had hastily wrapped in a paper table napkin, and set off again, this time for the green gate.

"She'll be back in about ten minutes," Georgie told Felicity, who was now sitting hunched up, rubbing her eyes with a small damp handkerchief. "Gerry doesn't get side-tracked, somehow. Six sandwiches, two each."

"I don't want any, thanks. I'd choke!"

"Try a small piece, then. Your grandmother will pass out if you collapse, as well as Susan."

"She wouldn't care. She's not my grandmother, anyway. She just has me here because there's nowhere else for me to go. I hate her!" Felicity muttered. "If she hadn't said Cherry Pie must be sold, I'd never have—never——" Tears were gathering again.

"Eat a sandwich," Georgie commanded, knowing that one can't do two things at once. "I'm beginning to think—to wonder—if you've stolen him yourself!"

Felicity's hand, outstretched to take the sandwich Georgie had broken in half for her, quivered and fell to her lap. "All right!" she said. "I did."

It was Georgie who nearly choked, for she had made her accusation at random, in an attempt to shake Felicity out of her lethargy. She had certainly done that.

"I'd promised Cherry I'd always keep him. He's been such a pet, always——"

"Always?" said Georgie. "How long have you had him?"

"Since I was seven. More than five years."

"But he must be too small for you, surely?"

"He wasn't! He was just right! And he always would have been, because I don't suppose I'll be very tall. And I could have had him as a pet, even if I couldn't ride him quite so much," Felicity said stubbornly, unaware that she was contradicting herself. "So I thought I'd hide him, you see, till I could make Grannie say that if only he'd come back he could stay for ever."

"But," asked Georgie, in amazement, "where on earth can one hide a pony?"

"In this garden," said Felicity. For the first time in their brief acquaintance, Georgie saw her smile. It was only a very faint glimmer, but it made a great difference. "I should say, *under* the garden," she added mysteriously.

"Under?" Georgie's head reeled, but she felt they were getting somewhere at last. She thought confusedly of disused tin mines, or subterranean caves. . . .

"You'll never guess. I'd never have guessed either, if Daddy hadn't shown me."

Then, bit by bit, the carefully guarded secret was told. Georgie, listening avidly, never thought of doubting it. Such a fantastic story must be true.

In the days of the Civil War, the Lord of the Manor who lived at Lebanon had given all he possessed to the Royalist cause. Not only did he organize the defence measures at the castle, but he undertook to provide fresh horses for the Cavaliers when the time came for the inevitable battle of Stonebridge. One batch of horses, temporarily out to grass, was stolen overnight. He remembered then that the house had been built with enormous cellars connecting with the castle by a series of underground passages. Could these be utilized now? he wondered. He discussed his idea with the cavalry experts, who were very enthusiastic. Miners from Cornwall, idle at the time, were sent secretly to Lebanon, and the cellars were enlarged and ventilated to make night quarters for a large number of horses. At least three new entrances were made. Two had disappeared, and no one knew where they had once been. But the third was in the garden now, Felicity declared, behind the high mossy bank not many yards from the arbour where they were sitting.

"But—but," said Georgie, staring at her incredulously, "you *can't* mean——?"

"Why not? They were meant for horses. I used to go down and feed him, and I'd put hay down there, and it wouldn't have been for long!" Felicity's eyes were full of tears again, but she wiped them away. "But he's vanished, you see. He didn't come last night when I called, and he hasn't come today. He's gone off into a dark corner and died of a broken heart."

"Or been removed by someone," said Georgie, waving to Gerry who had just reappeared at the green gate.

"But nobody *knows*!" Felicity insisted. "Daddy showed me the entrance because someone had shown him when he was a boy. That was the son of the old blacksmith, and Daddy said he'd been killed in the war, which meant that nobody knew about it, except Daddy and me. And now it's just me, or it was till a minute ago!"

"Well!" said Gerry, coming up to them and subsiding on one of the worn old seats, "everything's under control. Rough and Tough have promised to look out for Sorrel and see that the kids are all right, but of course they hope we'll be back before three."

"They must have wondered what we were doing," Georgie began, but her cousin shook her fair head.

"They were much too hungry. They'll come too, of course, later on." Gerry looked from Georgie to Felicity. "Now where have we got to?" she asked calmly, taking the two sandwiches which had been kept for her.

Felicity, after a little hesitation, repeated the extraordinary story she had just told Georgie, and the three sat in silence for a while. Then Georgie's thoughts flew to Spot, and she asked Gerry who was looking after him while the boys were having lunch.

"Terry Mulrany. They've got a groom there, and Spot's with Eileen Aroon. I believe that old major is nicer than he seems," said Gerry, "because he's asked where you are, several times, and told Rough he'd be responsible for Spot till you got back. He thinks we're visiting Sue, I suppose."

"You're wrong," said Felicity. "He's not nice! This is all his fault. *He* told Grannie that Cherry was too small for me, and got me into a row too. I told him he was wrong, and Grannie said I was rude, and wouldn't discuss it any more with me. Then I heard her phoning to Major Mulrany, something about deciding on a price, and—well, that made me do it. And now he's been smothered."

"Now don't start again," said Georgie and Gerry together, and Georgie went on, "That noise like thunder —was it you, banging something under the ground?"

"I was only shutting the door. It's a heavy one. I'm going back," Felicity said suddenly, springing up. "I must have one last look. I'll show you the entrance. I might as well, now it isn't a secret any more."

"Is it dark?" Gerry asked casually.

"We'll come all the way round with you, Felix, if you'll let us," Georgie said, at the same time, though she had turned rather pale. If Cherry Pie really had collapsed and died in there, Felicity ought not to be alone when she found him. She waited anxiously for the answer to Gerry's query.

"Not really dark, as long as there's daylight. It's the ventilation system. Daddy said they put shafts in somehow, to keep the air pure, and light comes down those. A lot of this garden is wild, you see, and always has been. I suppose it's just chance, that the tops of the shafts were never filled in. . . . Oh!" Felicity clapped both hands to her mouth. "Perkins has been pottering about the garden a lot lately. Perhaps he *has* filled them in, and that's why Cherry——"

Georgie felt a thrill of horror at the thought of the pony being suffocated. She jumped up.

"Let's go *now*," she said. "It's much better to know, and if he's ill, we might be in time to save him. What about water?"

"There's heaps down there. I filled up an old tank-thing that's been there for centuries. Oh, could that have poisoned him?" cried poor Felicity.

"Don't waste any more time," said Georgie, thinking this only too likely. Her heart sank like a stone when she realized what they might see.

Felicity stood up, looking like her old determined self again.

"Follow me," she said, "and remember, it's all shored up and perfectly safe. The only groggy thing is the entrance door, but I'll hold that for you."

Even the possibility of tragedy could not dim the excitement of that moment when the slight figure in stained jeans led Georgie and Gerry to the far side of the mossy bank, where it almost touched the old brick wall. Then Felicity lifted two lichened stones and revealed a most ordinary looking gap. She slipped her hand in this and found a lever, and the other girls saw that part of the bank was indeed a door, which slowly opened.

"This is hard work!" gasped Felicity. "It had to be opened wide for the horses, but we needn't open it so much. Oh! It's easier than I thought," she said, as the door moved with a jerk that nearly knocked Georgie down. "I had an awful job when I brought Cherry here a week ago."

A *week*! Well, of course, thought Georgie, remembering the account in the local paper, it must be a week since the pony disappeared. Was there the smallest chance of finding him alive? An uneven thumping sound startled her. It was the beating of her own heart.

"Buck up," said Felicity. "I'm holding the door for you, just in case it swings to. It feels looser, somehow."

Georgie wondered if Gerry felt this sense of utter panic which had all but paralysed her. They were standing in the lofty doorway, which measured roughly eight feet by six, and ahead of them loomed a wide passage lit dimly by the far-off sunshine which must be coming down those air shafts. But it smelt so cold and vault-like, and to the horrified eyes of the two visitors, it seemed to go on for ever.

"Come on!" said Gerry sharply. "We'll get the willies, standing here."

"All right," said Georgie, and they both stepped into the passage. It would be terribly easy to lose one's head here, and imagine all sorts of things. Like the sound of hoofs, for instance, and muttered commands, as the Cavaliers led out their brave horses to the battlefield.

"I'm shutting the door very carefully," Felicity said, behind them, "because it really does feel loose. *What's that?*"

Georgie and Gerry stiffened, their shoulders touching. They had heard it too, a queer little snuffling sound, and the tap of footsteps on the hard floor. They drew back involuntarily, till they were beside Felicity at the door. In another second all three were staring unbelievingly at the shape that loomed up in the eerie gloom.

Then Felicity gave a shriek. "Cherry!" she cried. "You're alive! But—what's happened? He's shrunk! He's half the size."

CHAPTER ELEVEN

DAYLIGHT

GEORGIE never forgot that lovely sight. One moment she had been oppressed by the gloom of her surroundings, and naturally dreading the discovery of a dead pony. The next, she found herself face to face with the prettiest toy horse that ever graced a Christmas bazaar. Daintily and without fear he came stepping towards them, a beautiful little colt of seven or eight weeks, his tiny, perfectly formed body perched on long legs, and his big bright eyes looking trustfully at the three silent humans. His unshod hoofs made the only sound in that strange place.

After that one wild outburst, Felicity seemed stricken dumb. But she opened the door again, to get more light, and as she did so the truth dawned upon them all. Georgie was the first to put it into words.

"He—he's Shrimpy, the strawberry roan!"

The little creature paused and blinked, and then snuffed again, joyfully. Wobbling slightly, he broke into a trot, brushing past them to get to the fresh air.

"Oh, no, you don't!" laughed Felicity, and made to shut the door. But Shrimpy was too quick for her. Out he went, and the door closed behind him with a reverberating thud. Felicity tried to open it, but it refused to budge.

"Give us a hand, will you?" she said rather jerkily. But the united efforts of all three were of no avail. The ancient door, already sagging on its hinges, had stuck at last.

"It isn't possible!" Gerry burst out. She went on tugging at the great wooden handle. "Why, nobody knows where we are!"

A deadly chill struck Georgie then. Supposing nobody *ever* knew where they were? Supposing the hours went by, and the days and months and years, till one day somebody found three skeletons—no, four, since Cherry Pie must be down here as well? She tried the handle herself, as Gerry gave up her attempt to move it; but the door was completely jammed. Nothing but a bulldozer could do the slightest good.

"Well," she said, as cheerfully as she could, "*one* person knows about this place, anyway. Probably three! You can see what they meant now, can't you, Gerry, when Sue heard them talking outside Cox's? I suppose one of them stole Shrimpy and put him in here, ready for the other to pick up and sell. But that must have been three days ago! One of them must have come, with milk and stuff for him; and *you* must have been coming too, Felix, to feed Cherry Pie. It's all such a hopeless muddle."

"I don't think it is," said Gerry, who was rapidly recovering her poise. "The thieves must have used one of the other entrances. Well, mustn't they? Just because your father didn't know where those entrances were, Felicity, it doesn't mean that nobody does! I think we'd better start hunting for the door they've been using."

"B-but they might come back and see us." Felicity faltered. "They might turn nasty."

"Not as nasty as staying down here for the rest of our lives," said Gerry. This was unanswerable.

"All right, then!" Georgie spoke bracingly, as her first shock began to wear off. "Let's explore the place now, while the light's still good. But we must keep together, and—— *What's that?*"

"It sounds like, it can't be——" Felicity gave a sudden sob. "It *is*! It's Cherry Pie!"

Tensely, they listened, and the queer distorted sound came again. A pony was whinnying somewhere on the same level as themselves. Felicity would have dashed forward, but Georgie seized her arm.

"We're keeping together, remember? We'll find him. Try calling his name."

Felicity called, and they heard him whinny and stamp. But that was all. It gave them only the vaguest idea of the direction they must take, but they set off, full of hope. They must have plodded up and down those earthy, twilit passages for twenty minutes before they found him. He was standing in a sort of blind alley, between crumbling walls, and his off foreleg was caught between two stones.

"You hold his head," Georgie said to Felicity, "and I'll try to get him free." And she knelt on the hard, cold earth, and managed to release the short, powerful leg. He lashed out the moment she succeeded, but she managed to avoid a kick. She could not see him very clearly, but she did just make out that he was a Shetland. He was, of course, very much too small for Felicity. She stroked his blunt face and felt the rasp of his tongue.

"He must be hungry," she said, "and, oh, golly, where's Gerry?"

"Here!" called a voice only a few yards away. "I was wondering if *this* could be the other entrance, where the stones are loose. If it hadn't been used for centuries, I suppose there could have been a bit of a landslide when the thieves came." She touched something and then darted back just in time, as several tons of earth crashed into the passage.

Rather shaken by her narrow escape, Gerry came back to the others.

"Whether it's the other entrance or not," she said, "it's much too dangerous to go near."

"Then we'll have to try to find the third one," Georgie said, with more confidence than she felt, and off they went again.

The little procession was slower now that Cherry Pie had joined it. Georgie and Gerry led the way, very cautiously, and Felicity followed with her pet, whose leg appeared to be quite all right. She had her arm round his neck, and they didn't look like a girl and her pony; but might have been a couple of friends strolling along hand-in-hand. Cherry Pie must have had a very bad scare, but he seemed quite content now that he was with Felicity again.

All the same, the three girls were very much aware that they could not go on walking like this for ever, or indeed for much longer. It was still quite early in the afternoon, but September days are short, and already the sunshine, coming down the hidden shafts, did not seem quite so strong.

Suddenly everything grew dark. Instinctively the three girls drew close together.

"The sun's gone in," said Gerry.

"Or else we're under the house," Georgie surmised, and then gave a cry. "Look! What on *earth* is that?"

Glancing round, she had suddenly noticed an oblong of dazzling light. It seemed to be above their heads, and not very far away, though this was impossible to judge in the gloom.

"What *is* it?" gasped Felicity. "What can it be? I've never been to this part of the stables before. It can't be a door, anyway . . ."

A door! That was what they were all longing for, with growing desperation. They could no longer see their watches, so time began to play tricks. Georgie's forehead was wet.

"Perhaps it's a skylight?" she ventured. "Let's try to get under it, shall we? It *might* give us some idea . . ."

"Come on, then. Anything's better than standing still!" Gerry said querulously. "I wish we could get some fresh air!"

Air! For the past ten minutes or so Georgie had been fighting against the realization that the atmosphere was becoming worse. Now she began to imagine terrible things, and failed to notice that the ground was rising until she suddenly fell flat on her face.

"Oh!" she gasped, as Gerry fell on top of her, and then they both scrambled to their feet. The oblong of light, which was now so much nearer, had suddenly taken on an almost familiar look. It seemed to be divided up into numerous little parallelograms.

"Why, they're diamonds!" she cried, as she and Gerry paused on the steep slope they were ascending. "Diamond panes. It's a *window*!"

"We must be at the old castle——" began Felicity; but Georgie and Gerry knew better. This was the secret of the seventh window at Lebanon. The excitement they felt then swept away their terror and weariness, and they fairly ran up the slope.

It was true. They had really solved the mystery. Georgie felt awe mixed with triumph, when she reached a rough kind of platform and gazed through glass at least three hundred years old. It was thin and clear, and not as dusty as one would have expected. Of course there must have been cobwebs, but luckily she did not think of those.

"Oh, Gerry, look!" she breathed. "This is the front of the house! There's the cedar! And there's the drive. And look, that old man with the barrow must be Perkins. Let's shout!"

"As if he could hear!" snorted Gerry. "We'll have to break the glass. Or at least, Felicity's the one to do that. Where is she?"

"Here!" said Felicity, from below. "I can't get Cherry Pie to walk up. Well, he'll just have to wait for us, that's all!"

She came up herself, and joined the others. In the brilliant daylight, which was still hurting their eyes, they saw how wan and pale she looked.

"O.K.," she said, "I'll break the middle pane."

It seemed a dreadful thing to do, but they were forced ito it. She took off one shoe, and there was a musical tinkle as the thin glass shattered. Georgie and Gerry saw the old man with the barrow look up in utter stupefaction.

"Fetch Grannie!" shouted Felicity. "*Please* fetch Grannie!" And, shaking his head helplessly, Perkins went off to do so.

Now that the first thrill had subsided, Georgie began to wonder how this adventure would end. They had reached the window and summoned help, but the window was too small for a girl to get through, let alone a rather portly Shetland pony. They were still prisoners.

But Gerry, of course, had the situation in hand. When Perkins did bring old Mrs. Brown to see this astonishing sight, Gerry was the first to speak.

"Good afternoon," she said politely, through the jagged hole in the glass. "We three are in the old stables which runs underneath the house. We came through a doorway in the mossy bank by your green outer door, which has now collapsed. So will you please get the police?"

"The Driscoe police!" put in Georgie, thinking that one village constable wouldn't be much good.

"Yes!" said Felicity. "Driscoe 124. I shan't forget *that* number," she added under her breath.

Mrs. Brown was not a person to waste time over foolish questions. She realized that the girls were in deadly earnest.

"I shall ring the police immediately," she said, "and you can explain yourselves later. Stables! A doorway in the bank!" She limped away with surprising rapidity.

"Thank goodness she understood!" said Georgie. "Now we must just wait again. Gerry!"

"*I'm* not pushing!" said Gerry indignantly. "Sorry if I'm on your toe, but Felicity pushed me. She—why, she's gone!"

"I'm looking for Cherry Pie!" Felicity called from below. "I suddenly thought of him, and he's wandered off!"

"Well, don't you wander after him——" Georgie began, and then realized that Felicity had done just that. "She must be daft!" Georgie went on wrathfully. "She'll get lost again. I shall just go and bring her back, that's all. Cherry Pie won't go far."

"Georgie! No!" cried Gerry, but Georgie, edging her way down the slope, only laughed.

"*I* won't get lost. I'll keep watching the window," she said, and at once began to look for Felicity. She could hear her, but that was all. Moreover, looking into the darkness again after facing the bright daylight made Georgie's eyes water badly. She felt for her handkerchief and mopped them vigorously. It was then that she must have taken the wrong turning, for when she next looked round she saw no trace of the window. Neither had she found Felicity.

This was the worst part of the adventure, and it seemed to go on for hours. Georgie called till she was hoarse, and she could hear Felicity calling Cherry Pie. Gerry who was still sensibly by the window, of course, called everyone in turn, but it was just like being in a maze. At last, after what seemed hours, Georgie came face to face with Cherry Pie. She caught him, digging her cold fingers into his mane.

She was aware now of a different sound. Footsteps. Men's footsteps, drawing nearer and nearer. The police? Or the thieves?

She shrank against the clammy wall, still gripping Cherry Pie, and waited in fascinated horror as the first of the torches appeared, like flashing eyes. Then a deep, familiar voice spoke out in friendly astonishment. "Blow me down," it said, "if it isn't Mr. Kane's daughter from Dockleford! Well, I never!"

It was the voice of Twinkletoes.

He had been at the Driscoe police station when the message came, and had had a place in the car which

"Blow me down, if it isn't Mr. Kane's daughter from Dockleford!"

sped to the rescue. The police had found the entrance quite easily, and had broken the old door down with crowbars. With their powerful torches they soon located poor Felicity, who had been trailing round in circles, and Gerry, who had not budged from the window. And soon the captives were set free. Cherry Pie, almost blinded by the daylight, bucked and reared at first till he got his bearings. Then, shaking off Felicity's hand, he galloped off to the paddock to taste the joys of liberty, just as the Cavaliers' horses must have done, all those years ago.

Georgie, Gerry, and Felicity came forward rather sheepishly to be questioned by old Mrs. Brown, who was waiting for them in the arbour, leaning on her stick. It had been such a weird adventure, fraught with so much anxiety and fear, that they all felt it had lasted much longer than it had. Georgie glanced at her watch, and gasped. It wasn't much after tea-time even now!

"Grannie," Felicity said bravely, though she looked ready to faint, "I hid him in there. I didn't want you to sell him to strangers. I did it to make you sorry. I wanted to make you say I could keep him if he ever came back."

The old lady looked at her keenly.

"You should trust me better than that," she said. "I'd never have let him go to strangers. Some friends in Cornwall were to have had him for their two small children, and they love ponies, and you could have visited him whenever you liked. And Major Mulrany was going to let me have Eileen Aroon for you, as Terry has to go abroad to join his parents. But I don't know now. The Cornish family have bought another Shetland for their twins, and the Major's had several offers for Eileen. I'm not reproaching you, Felicity, I'm just trying to explain. It was to have been a lovely surprise for you."

"Oh—Oh, I'm sorry, Grannie. I've been a pig!" gasped Felicity, while the other two looked at her in sympathy.

"No, my dear—only pig-headed," was the calm reply. "You've behaved very wrongly, and we must talk about it afterwards. But your father and mother would have been proud of you," Mrs. Brown said deliberately, "just as I am. Now come in and wash, all of you, and make your peace with Susan, who has guessed that something's been going on."

"I'm afraid we shall have to come in too, ma'am," said a kindly middle-aged policeman who turned out to be none other than Sergeant Green! "We must question the young ladies, and maybe I owe someone an apology," he added handsomely.

He turned out to be very nice, and in the course of the questioning, which took a long time, he explained about the misunderstanding which had made him refuse to speak to them on the telephone. He asked permission to interview Susan, who was the only one who had actually *seen* the horse thieves, and assured the anxious girls that Shrimpy would be found.

Mrs. Brown gave everyone tea, and Susan managed to tell Georgie that she was having a very good time.

"Though I'll be jolly glad to be back at Wychwood," she added hastily. "How are you going, by the way? And what about Spot? And the Lads? And——?"

"I don't know, Sue. There's been so much going on. But it's only just six o'clock," said Georgie, "and if Gerry's game, I'd like to go back to the Show!"

CHAPTER TWELVE

THE END OF IT ALL . . .

GEORGIE and Gerry were more tired than they realized, and it seemed quite a long way to walk back to the Plain. Mrs. Brown made them promise to come back to Lebanon Lodge, if no satisfactory arrangements could be made for their journey home; but that part turned out to be quite simple. As soon as they reached the Plain, where the Show was being dismantled, the boys told them that Miss Mitton, owner of the poodle Matilda, had offered to drive them all home, and would call for Susan as well. So that was all right.

"Don't let's tell any of these people about Cherry Pie or the underground stables," Georgie said to Gerry in a low voice, as they entered the enclosure where Spot was waiting with some other ponies and horses. "It's such a big adventure that it would take all night to describe. Everyone will know about it soon, but not just yet! Oh, Gerry! To think that *we've* solved the mystery!"

Gerry smiled. "It *was* pretty bright of us," she said modestly, "and you're right about not telling people yet. It *would* take too long, and besides, it's Felicity's story in a way."

To their surprise, nobody asked them where they

had been all this time. The Show had been going on until about half an hour ago, and it had been packed with incidents.

"How did Sorrel get on?" Georgie asked Mrs. Davis, who began to laugh. It seemed that Sorrel had done very well. She had won the second prize in the Veterans' Parade, and Frankie Carson and his brothers and sisters had gone home the richer by five pounds. But what was even better than that was the fact that Shrimpy had rejoined his mother just after her triumph. Some people had found the little fellow wandering on the main road, and had wisely brought him to the Show. Once there, of course, he had been led up to Sorrel, who had kicked up her heels for joy. Both mother and son were now safely back at Kingfisher Farm, and Major Mulrany told Georgie that he had asked the Carsons to telephone Farmer Leadbetter and tell him not to worry about fetching Spot.

"I shall be happy to keep him overnight, and have him brought back to you in the morning," he said. "And don't forget to take your box of chocolates with you, Georgie Kane. They tell me you've only been riding since January. If that's so, you've done well, and we shall be hearing more of you."

The unexpected compliment left Georgie speechless, but her delight showed in her face. What a wonderful day it had been! But now it was over, and it was very difficult not to fall asleep inside Miss Mitton's car. Georgie had only one clear memory of that drive home, and that was seeing the last golden finger of sunset touching the secret window at Lebanon.

When she woke up next morning her head was still full of all the exciting things that had happened. Spot returned soon after breakfast, and it was really funny to see him gallop up to the stolid Timbo the moment he was put back into the field.

Susan had quite recovered by now, and came down to breakfast as hungry as ever. Luckily there were plenty of eggs, but as no one had had any time to go shopping yesterday, the girls would have to open some tins for lunch.

"And we must remember to leave enough food for Mother and Daddy and the Duponts," Georgie said in housewifely tones. "I wonder what time they'll arrive?"

"Mother said, soon after tea, when she rang me up last night," said Peter, overhearing this. "I forgot to tell you. She said the Duponts want to stay in England for a few years, and are looking out for a small, quiet pony for their children." And he raised his brows inquiringly as Georgie and Gerry exchanged looks of glee.

They all went to the morning service at the village church, and when it was over the vicar walked to the gate with them, and asked if the beds had arrived safely. As she thanked him, Georgie thought that the adventure had really started when those beds had turned up at Wychwood in Farmer Leadbetter's Noah's Ark. It seemed quite a month ago.

"This time yesterday," Susan remarked as they walked up the drive, "you and I were just about visiting Lebanon for the first time. Do you remember how Felicity brought me that stale cake? I wondered where she'd got it from. It must have been part of the store she kept for Cherry Pie."

"The whole thing seems utterly fantastic!" said Gerry, with a return to her superior manner. "You see, Georgie, it *was* one of your own brand of adventures, all that flapping, and tearing about, and nothing to show at the end! All the same, I do wonder when we shall hear what happened about those horse thieves?"

They did hear very soon, almost at once, in fact. The telephone was ringing when they entered the house. It was a call for Georgie from Felicity Brown.

"I thought you'd like to know," said the remembered voice, "that Cherry Pie's perfectly all right after all he's been through, and Grannie says he can stay here till we find some really good home for him. And if we do find one I'm really going to have Eileen Aroon!"

"That will be super, Felix!"

"I'm longing for next year's Show already! Oh, by the way, the thieves have been caught."

"Have they? Tell me, quickly," cried Georgie. "Do you know yet how they found out about the entrance?"

That was one of the most baffling parts of the whole thing, she thought, and she listened avidly while Felicity told her the facts.

Felicity's father had assumed that, since the blacksmith's son had been killed in the war, nobody but himself knew of that secret entrance in the mossy bank. But he had not realized that the blacksmith's son had a son of his own, who had been told about it, and remembered. He was a lazy, worthless type of youth, and when he made friends with two others, worse than himself, he became a thief. He saw little Shrimpy one day when he was passing Kingfisher Farm, and at once recognized his value. He told the others, and somehow they hatched a scheme whereby the colt would be stolen and hidden by one of the gang, and picked up later by another. But the question was, where could one hide a lively colt, and at the same time visit him and feed him until he could be taken away?

Then this man remembered the old story of the hidden stables at Lebanon. His father had once shown him where the door was supposed to be. He went to have a look and found it all too easily. By one of those strange coincidences which so frequently occur, Felicity had been using the door that very week.

So Shrimpy was kidnapped and put into that eerie place. Unknown to his captors, he must have met Cherry Pie. Georgie wondered what would have happened if the thieves had come face to face with the old Shetland instead of the strawberry roan! Perhaps the two ponies had hobnobbed in those murky depths, and compared notes upon the peculiar habits of the human race. No one would ever know . . .

"They were on their way to fetch Shrimpy," Felicity said, "when you saw them in the bus. One of them had hired a van which was to meet them after dark, when they would smuggle him out. The garage people had thought there was something queer going on, so when the van wasn't collected they told the police. And that was how the thieves were caught so quickly. Isn't it thrilling? But not so thrilling as that window! That story will be in the *Echo*, I'm sure, because we had the same silly man round just now, asking Grannie and me all about it."

"What did he say about the reappearance of Cherry Pie?" Georgie asked rather diffidently, and there was a pause at the other end of the line.

"Well," Felicity answered carefully, at last, "Grannie has asked him not to let on what really happened, but just to mention that he's been found. That ought not to be difficult, when the window story is so much more interesting to ordinary people. Grannie really has been decent about all this. It's funny, but after all this I sort of feel she is my *real* grandmother."

"And so you jolly well should!" said Georgie bracingly. "I do hope you'll get Eileen Aroon. I think you will, somehow! Good-bye, Felix. Pat Cherry Pie for me, and ask him if he speaks French!"

The girls were very busy that afternoon, making up the spare beds and hunting out old toys, as there had been no time or enough money to spare, to buy new ones. When everything was done, Georgie went to the field to see Spot, who looked very pleased with himself. It was too late to saddle him, so she just talked to him for a while, and gave him three of the chocolates Major Mulrany had given her. Spot munched them solemnly and Georgie, looking into his lovely bright eyes, wondered if he could be dreaming, as she was, of future shows and gymkhanas, and the hazards they would tackle together.

Then, as the autumn wind grew cold, she went back to the house and paused on the threshold of the sitting-room. The others had not heard her approach, and so she was able to stand there for a little while and look at the familiar scene. Peter was reading, of course. Gerry, in her favourite straight-backed chair, was getting on with her embroidery. Rough and Tough, on the floor, were completely absorbed in teaching their spaniels a complicated trick. On the settee Susan was practising her recorder behind a sound barrier of cushions.

"Why," thought Georgie, "it all looks exactly the same as it did on Thursday evening, before we knew about the Duponts' accident, or the Stonebridge Show, or that scrap of paper Sue picked up. It's almost as if the whole adventure—what did we call it? A Puzzle of Ponies!—had been just a dream."

After all, as Gerry had pointed out, it had been one of those adventures with nothing to show at the end. Nothing except fun and thrills, danger and fear, and the faces of new friends.

Georgie scooped up King Toby, who had joined her and was using her ankle as a pincushion, and joined the others by the fire.

The Armada Quiz and Puzzle Books Nos. 1-5

Boost your brain power and have hours of puzzling fun solving the hundreds of different quizzes in this popular Armada series.

Pick your favourite puzzle – names, pictures, anagrams, codes, magic squares, pets, mysteries, sport, history, spelling, doodles, and many, many more. Sharpen your wits and get puzzling!

Have you discovered Armada's latest quiz books? Facts and fun for everyone in six exciting titles:

The Armada Horse & Pony Quiz Books Nos. 1 & 2
by Charlotte Popescu

The Armada Football Quiz Books Nos. 1 & 2
by Gordon Jeffery

The Armada Animal Quiz Book
by Deborah Holder

Car Quiz
by Hal Danby